KATIE AND PETER
TOO MUCH IN LOVE

KATIE AND PETER
TOO MUCH IN LOVE

E M I L Y   H E R B E R T

JOHN BLAKE

Published by Metro Publishing
an imprint of John Blake Publishing Ltd
3 Bramber Court, 2 Bramber Road,
London W14 9PB, England

www.johnblakepublishing.co.uk

First published in paperback in 2009

ISBN: 978 1 84454 868 2

British Library Cataloguing-in-Publication Data:

A catalogue record for this book is available from the British Library.

Printed in Great Britain by CPI Bookmarque, Croydon CR0 4TD

1 3 5 7 9 10 8 6 4 2

Papers used by John Blake Publishing are natural, recyclable products made from
wood grown in sustainable forests. The manufacturing processes conform to the
environmental regulations of the country of origin.

All photographs reproduced by Rex Features, except where indicated.

CONTENTS

CHAPTER ONE

THE END OF A DREAM

The news, when it broke, was a shock. One minute one of the most famous duos in the country, Katie Price and Peter Andre, seemed to be the happiest of couples, helping one another through the London Marathon, and giggling about going to bed afterwards, and how much they fancied one another, and the next, the relationship was over. Just like that. A quite spectacular row had taken place, in which words were said that shouldn't have been said and insults flung that couldn't be forgotten, but, whereas most couples go through such moments and try to forget about it afterwards, in this particular case, it was all caught on television cameras. Even if Katie and Peter had managed to put their massive argument behind them, the rest of the world would still be around to witness all the mess.

But then, as events began to unfold, it soon became clear

that this row, and the subsequent separation, had been a long time in the making. Various elements were about to emerge – from the lyrics of songs Peter had written months earlier to totally unfounded rumours that Katie might have been having an affair – that made it clear that the couple's relationship had been in turmoil for a long time. The split, it seemed, had become inevitable. The relationship that the whole nation had seen develop years earlier on *I'm A Celebrity... Get Me Out of Here!*, where the two first met, was over, and in the most acrimonious of circumstances, too.

It was a long way from the couple's lavish wedding day, at Highclere Castle, less than four years earlier, and the announcement that the pair of them issued on 11 May 2009 in the wake of the revelation that they were to part could not have been more blunt: 'Peter Andre and Katie Price are separating after four-and-a-half years of marriage [sic],' they said. 'They have both requested the media respect their families' privacy at this difficult time.'

So, what had gone wrong? In the immediate aftermath of the split, it was not clear what had happened, other than that Peter was the one who had packed his bags and left, rather than Katie, but no one could work out why. In a highly emotional statement, Katie said, 'Pete is the love of my life. We have children together and I am devastated and disappointed by his decision to separate and divorce me, as I married him for life. This is not what I want and the decision has been taken out of my hands. I will not comment further or do any interviews regarding the separation, but I will always love my Pete.'

The timing was extraordinary. Days earlier, Katie had announced they were hoping for another child. 'Hopefully, I will get pregnant next year as we are going to start trying,' she said. 'I want to have another three kids biologically and then adopt, but, if something happened and there was a child who needed a home before that, then I'd do it.'

This was hardly the talk of a woman on the verge of getting divorced. Then there was the fact that she'd just made an impromptu visit to Los Angeles, where Pete was recording an album, and during which he'd seemed overjoyed to see her – although, as was shortly to become apparent, the couple had had a terrible row when she was there. Indeed, rumours had started to circulate that the marriage was in trouble. But, when questioned about it at BAA Heathrow, on her way home, Katie was adamant nothing was wrong. 'As usual, it's a load of nonsense,' she said.

During the trip, the couple had been spotted kissing passionately, after which waiting photographers asked them about their plans for the evening.

'Do you know what? I'm going to have fun with her,' said Pete.

But this was not enough to silence the talk. One source

close to the couple remarked, 'It's going from bad to worse for them,' while another said that they were treating Pete's working trip to LA as a trial separation, as both tried to determine what they really wanted next.

However, the separation soon turned from a trial into the real thing and it wasn't long before the whole story began to emerge. In fact, the full extent of the couple's problems became clear when the huge row between them was broadcast on their ITV2 reality show, *Katie & Peter: The Next Chapter – Stateside*. It started innocuously enough, as such rows so often do, until the pair were quite suddenly in the middle of something so blisteringly ferocious neither seemed able to climb down. Was it the end? Yes. There really seemed to be no going back from there.

It came about as follows. Katie and Pete were in a shop having a seemingly casual conversation about nothing very much, when it suddenly blew up into a row about which one of them the shop assistant recognised. 'When someone knows who you are and you come into a shop and you're blatantly lying, you look a twat,' snapped Katie.

'Really? Shhh, Kate, zip it,' said Pete, before turning to the shop assistant. 'So, have you heard of Kate?'

'I'm not sure,' replied the rather bemused assistant.

'How do you feel now?' demanded Pete, turning back to Katie. 'How do *you* feel?'

Although neither said as much, the whole slanging match reeked of being an argument the duo had had many times before. Who was the more famous – did it really matter? But to Katie, at least, it clearly did. When the two of them first met, much was made of the fact that Pete was well past his glory days, while Katie, then widely known as the glamour model Jordan, was by far the more famous one. As a couple, their joint profile totally dwarfed any fame either had had before then, but which of the two was now individually more famous was impossible to say. But, if that had previously been a bone of contention, it was now spinning totally out of control.

The row continued, becoming increasingly bad-tempered as it did so.

'You're a fucking knob. I can't stand you!' said Katie.

'Ahh, did I hurt your feelings?' asked Pete. 'Did he not know who you were?'

'Oh, as if I'm bothered,' said Katie. 'No one knows who you are. You're an old fucking singer no one knows about!'

That was vicious, but matters swiftly got worse.

'You've got a real attitude problem,' said Pete, who was looking increasingly riled.

'Get over it, Pete. I want to go home!' said Katie.

'I'm so glad you guys are here to film this,' said Pete, turning to the film crew.

'I'm so glad too, so you know what a knob you are,' was Katie's response.

'You can see what kind of a stupid, miserable, arrogant cow she is,' said Pete, who was by now giving every

5

appearance of a man who had heard it all before and had well and truly had enough.

'Arrogant? What, 'cos I'm talking to someone genuinely and you're sitting there, fucking lying? I can't stand liars,' Katie continued.

'*Really?* You've got fucking issues,' said Pete. 'I can't wait for you to watch this back and see how miserable you are.'

Could things get any more unpleasant than that? Oh, yes – and they did.

Pete accused Katie of trying to have it all her own way, to which Katie retorted, '*I'm* the one making money, Pete, so of course I can have it how I want.'

It clearly wounded him to the core. 'What? Don't I make money?' he demanded.

'I don't know. Do you? Hurts, doesn't it?' Katie replied.

'How fucking dare you talk to me like that! Think you're gonna get away with it?' demanded Pete.

At this point, clearly realising this was going too far, one of the couple's management team, Nicola Partridge, stepped in. But it was too late, not least because everything had been captured on camera and the footage was due to be screened the following week. Katie and Pete were livid with one another and no longer prepared to hide it any more. And so, a bitter breakdown between the two of them had really begun.

It wasn't exactly *Love's Young Dream*, but then rumours had been circulating for some time that all was not well. The previous night, Katie had been spotted without Pete at Syndicate nightclub in Bristol, where she was photographed whispering to a mystery man, leading to much speculation as to who he was and the exact nature of their relationship. As if that was not enough, she sang a not entirely successful version of Pete's hit 'Mysterious Girl'.

But, until practically the day before the split, Katie had been keen to emphasise that the two were very happy. It made the suddenness of the break all the more incomprehensible, because until extremely recently the couple had appeared to be so very much in love.

This was illustrated by an interview she gave in March 2009, in which she revealed to Piers Morgan that, shortly after Pete was booted off *I'm A Celebrity...*, she asked him to marry her. 'I said to him, "The letter 'm' – it's Leap Year. Will you, will you?" He said, "*What*, marry?" Now I couldn't be happier with Peter. He's stuck around for five years, so I can't be *that* bad.'

That was only two months before the split was announced: matters had gone very wrong, very fast – in public, at least. However, Katie's comment 'I can't be *that* bad' hinted that something more was going on behind the scenes. Many believe that the problems Katie has with relationships stem from the fact that she doesn't really love herself: the throwaway remark certainly supported that theory.

So, the two would actually split? Certainly, the news came as a surprise to Katie's stepfather, Paul Price, who lives in Ditchling, East Sussex, where he runs a fencing firm. He appeared to be taken aback when he found out what was happening. 'I've been at work. I haven't heard anything or spoken to anyone about it,' he told one reporter. 'I'm surprised. I'll give her a call and find out what's happening. I can't say any more because I don't know anything. But whatever they do is their business, isn't it?'

And it might well have been, but the whole country was fascinated, too. Ever since that first meeting in the Australian jungle in 2004, and especially since their wedding, in which Katie appeared as every little girl's dream vision of a fairytale bride, Katie and Pete had become a couple of such interest to the public that they even rivalled the Beckhams. Perhaps the break-up was their business, but that didn't mean that everyone else didn't want to know what was going on, too.

One problem did seem to be jealousy. Katie always attracted a huge amount of male attention, which Pete hated, and those pictures of her out in Bristol appeared to be the last straw. 'She's rubbing my face in it – she knows her behaviour is out of order,' he told a friend.

Sources close to the couple revealed that he had always found it hard to deal with all the attention his wife got, even when he was actually there. 'Peter knew that going out with Jordan would attract jealous glances,' said one. 'He hated her going out and getting drunk. He was also jealous of the male attention that follows her and told her so. She, on the other hand, was driven mad by his jealousy but at the end of the day they always kissed and made up. However, it got too much for him. It's very sad.'

Of course, Pete, although he was brought up in Australia, is of Cypriot stock and Mediterranean men are often known to have a hot-blooded streak in them. In the circles he originally moved in, it did not do to have people ogling your wife, and he clearly found it very difficult to deal with this. But then, even before the two of them got together, Katie had been a glamour model, and Pete knew that. It was, perhaps, simply more difficult to deal with all that that brought with it than he'd first realised.

Certainly, Katie often found it hard to handle her husband's possessiveness, although she admitted to being guilty of fits of jealous rage, too. 'He thought I was always flirting and interested in other men,' she conceded. 'And, if I'm honest, I thought he was doing the same, too. It's just too draining.'

That the relationship was a volatile one had been obvious for some time now, but both were beginning to feel they could no longer handle it. The rows were getting too far out of control.

And so Pete finally walked out, after which matters reached an impasse. Amid reports that Katie was asking him to reconsider his decision to leave, Pete went to stay with his brother, Mike, while Katie took the couple's three children, Junior (three), Princess Tiáamii (21 months) and Harvey, Katie's severely disabled six-year-old son from her relationship with footballer Dwight Yorke, to a private home away from the eyes of the cameras.

It was increasingly obvious that this latest argument had been one in a long series of rows from which the couple had always previously recovered, but which this time had been allowed to get completely out of hand.

But there were numerous reasons why matters finally came to a head. One of the problems seemed to be the occasions when Katie would have a few drinks, which made her uninhibited and often had her lashing out verbally. Both had spoken about it in the past, with Pete publicly admitting it made him worry about what Katie might do after a drink. At the very least, it could bring out that harsh tongue. 'I'm not jealous of anybody until Katie's drunk. There's nobody I feel threatened by when she's sober. If she's been drinking, I know she's capable of anything,' he said. 'The Devil gets inside her and she's a nightmare.'

Increasingly, however, attention was focused on that night out in the Bristol club, when she did appear to have been drinking. Ironically, it emerged that the mystery man Katie had been seen chatting to was, in fact, gay. Spencer Wilton, a 35-year-old international dressage rider, put matters straight in *Horse & Hound* magazine: 'A big group of us had all been at Badminton Horse Trials for the day, and went out for dinner afterwards and on to a club,' he said. 'They [the media] know exactly who I am and have chosen to ignore that and the fact that I'm already in a happy relationship with a male partner. My phone hasn't stopped with papers and magazines calling, but it's obviously a lot worse for Katie – I just really hope she and Peter are able to resolve their differences.'

To make the point, his former lover Carl Hester also spoke out. 'They are absolutely not having an affair of any sort,' said Hester, a 40-year-old three-time Olympian dressage rider. 'He has a new partner that he lives with – a man named Jay. I saw them all together in the day; it was just a big group of people having fun. It's out of the realms of possibility – Spencer's gay. Katie knows his partner as well and Spencer's good friends with Katie's trainer, so they were all there together.'

This was clearly someone Pete had no need to be jealous of, but it was too late: the damage was already done.

As the story dominated the front pages, many snippets from the past began to appear, too, shedding a new light on the relationship and the stresses and strains that had finally brought it to a halt. The extent of Pete's jealousy became apparent when Rebecca Loos, of all people, entered the debate. The one-time alleged paramour of David Beckham told the *Daily Star* of an occasion some years previously when Pete suspected Rebecca of having designs on his wife.

'I was at Andrew Wong's Chinese New Year party in 2006 and I got chatting to Katie and Peter,' Rebecca said. 'They were really lovely. I remember Kate and I went to the toilet and did our make-up together. She was pissed and I was pissed... We put our make-up and lipstick on. Then we came out and started dancing together. It was all completely innocent, we were just having a laugh. The next thing I know is that Pete is convinced I made a pass at Kate in the bathroom. Nothing could be further from the truth. I'm not nearly as bad as people think I am.'

It might have seemed a ludicrous accusation, yet Pete had been certain something was going on. 'Kate was so smashed she didn't have a clue what was going on,' he said at the time. 'Rebecca kept asking her to go to the toilet because girls always go together. I had this horrible feeling she was taking advantage of Kate. It can't take that long to powder your nose.'

In the event, of course, nothing occurred, but it was a sign of quite how upset Pete could allow himself to become.

Reports continued to circulate that Katie wanted a reconciliation but Pete was adamant there was no going back. Friends revealed that he'd told her, 'It's over between us. All I care about now are the kids.'

A source close to the estranged couple said it was very tense: 'They are still civil and talking but it's all about their children now. He refuses to talk about the status of their relationship, which is really upsetting Katie. It's not World War Three, but you wouldn't want to see them in the same house together. Peter has been telling his brother that he's looking forward to being a single man again; there are lots of very different emotions running through his head. But he's glad it's finally out there in the open and he can look to the future. He still cares for Katie but his priority is seeing his children.'

Worn down by the rowing, it seemed Pete was starting to see matters in a new light.

As time went on, it became increasingly apparent that the split was no sudden whim. Matters had been slowly going wrong. For some time, Pete had been working on material for a new album, *Control*, and lyrics came to light that he'd written as far back as November 2008. They painted a very revealing picture of his state of mind, particularly the song 'Call Me A Doctor', in which he referred to walking away from his relationship and expressing regret at having had anything to do with the woman in question.

In the *Sun*, Pete confirmed that he had indeed been referring to Katie in the song and, in fact, it is hard to see who else might have fitted that particular bill. Songwriting is a notoriously personal activity, and it seemed as if this might have been one way for Pete to deal with the pain.

Another track on the same album, 'Replay', also talked about the pain of love going wrong and the desire to start out afresh. But now it was too late: neither could go back to where they used to be. Matters had gone too far for that.

Until now, there had been much speculation about what would happen with the children. The two younger ones were the natural children of both, while Pete had formed a strong bond with Harvey, bringing him up as his own. Where would they all go now? Who would care for them? The problems that arose out of this particular dilemma soon became apparent as both tried to cheer themselves up in the immediate aftermath of the split: Katie flew to the Maldives in May for a break, taking Junior and Princess Tiáamii with her and leaving Harvey in the UK to be looked after by his professional carer and various other family members, including, she seemed to think, Pete.

There were reports that Pete was very hurt by her behaviour as the Maldives was where the couple had spent their honeymoon. Perhaps as a result of this, he went to stay with family at his luxury villa in Cyprus, while Harvey was cared for at his special-needs school. A fresh war of words broke out.

Katie was livid that, as she saw it, Pete had left Harvey alone, something that promptly made matters considerably worse. 'Can you believe Pete's fucked off, leaving Harvey home alone?' she is said to have demanded of friends. 'He's just packed up his shit and gone! He's acting like a complete knob. How dare he? If this is how it's going to be from now on, then so be it.'

In actual fact, Katie and Peter are both devoted and caring parents who would never do anything that would mean their kids were anything other than extremely well cared for.

But Pete was equally upset. 'All hell has broken loose,' said a source close to the couple. 'Family means everything to Pete and so the fact his two natural kids are with Kate on the other side of the world is a killer blow. He's saddened by her choice of destination as it holds so many memories of happier days. If she's gone off to have a good time, then so will he. He's gone to stay with his brothers in Cyprus and he's going to be living it up. He couldn't take Harvey out of his special-needs school, so he left him with his carer and Kate's mum. Katie is incandescent as she wanted him to stay put in Surrey, instead of swanning off at what seems like the drop of a hat. Both parties are livid with the other and they both feel they are in the right. It's a no-win situation.'

It certainly was that. Nor did it help that Pete was initially pictured looking relaxed, although his demeanour became increasingly sombre as the days wore on; he was staying at his villa in Pervolia, near Larnaca, with his brothers Michael and Chris, along with two male friends, where they were seen having a barbecue and swimming. These were hardly images guaranteed to calm Katie down, although in reality the strain was beginning to take its toll on Pete quite as much as it was on her.

By this time Pete's father, Savvas Andrea, had also heard the news. Describing Katie as 'the perfect daughter-in-law', Savvas was clearly distressed, hoping the couple would get back together again. 'It has come as a complete shock to all the family,' he said. 'I haven't spoken to Peter since the news broke. The first we heard about it was when the story came on the television. I thought it was a joke at first. It must be temporary. They love each other too much to break up for good. I think in about a month they'll be back together. I have a gut feeling about it. Peter must be really upset because I would have expected him to call me by now. I think he has just gone somewhere to think things through by himself.'

But, in doing so, much as he missed his children, it was becoming increasingly clear to him that the relationship had now come to an end.

Everyone, it seemed, was shaken. By now, messages were pouring in from fans. 'Hi guys,' wrote Katie on Twitter, which was how she kept up with people when she was in the Maldives. 'Thank you for all your support. It means so much to me.'

Attention began to focus on another bone of contention – money. It had been Katie's jibes about Pete's earning capacity that had finally driven the two of them to go over the top in their much-publicised row. Now there was speculation that she might have to make a large payout. Katie was worth an estimated £40 million by this point, not a sum to be sniffed at. But Pete wouldn't even countenance the thought of it. 'I don't want your millions,' he told her, before adding to friends, 'I wouldn't get a penny if we broke up because I signed a pre-nuptial – and it was my idea to do it. I insisted on it beforehand.'

Certainly, Pete didn't seem keen on causing trouble financially. It was clear that, underneath it all, he was a fundamentally upright guy. The values of his traditional upbringing had stayed with him, and, much as he might have found it difficult to live their married life in Katie's shadow, he clearly showed no sign of wanting to take advantage of her financially following the break-up. There was speculation that he could expect up to £6 million, half of the estimated £12 million they were thought to have made since the marriage, but friends were adamant that he wouldn't go after anything more.

'Say what you want about Peter, he is a good guy and integrity and honesty are important to him. He's from a good family, with proper values, and, when you meet his folks, you understand the man. A lot of people in music, especially those who, like Pete, had success when they were really young, are conceited and arrogant,' commented a friend. 'But Pete's not like that. He's got no ego on him to speak of. If anything, he lacks confidence in his ability and doesn't realise what a good musician he is. He's a really decent guy who has had to put up with some of his wife's excesses and occasional coarseness because he loves her.'

And in that lay the true sadness of it all, for the couple really had been in love and the fact that their relationship had gone wrong was shattering to both. But their lives were also increasingly going in opposite directions: their sets of friends were different, and, while Pete was showing signs of wanting to stay in LA, Katie was keen to go home to her huge house in the country and her horses. And the fact that both had volatile personalities meant that they wound one another up, rather than calming each other down.

But both were clearly devastated by it all. Pete's troubled state of mind was borne out by those who were spending time with him. His friend Nikos Christophi, a restaurant owner, who spent some time with him in the Cypriot villa reported afterwards, 'He's not over the moon. Peter's very sad and quiet.' Indeed, he'd told Nikos he was increasingly worried about his future with the children, adding, 'The kids mean everything to me. They are my life.'

In fact, far from living it up, as perhaps Katie suspected him of doing, Peter was cutting an increasingly melancholic figure. Another aspect of his Cypriot upbringing, of course, is that divorce is far less common than it is in northern European countries. Clearly, this was all coming as a terrible shock. And, even though tensions had evidently been building for some time, the end of any relationship, no matter how public or private, is still a dreadful blow. The full impact of what was happening was now becoming plain.

Another aspect of the relationship where there had clearly been difficulties was the physical one. Far from being all over each other, it seems that, by the time the relationship finally broke down, Katie and Pete had not had sex for four months. Not only was this a sign that something was seriously wrong in the relationship, to a macho man like Pete it would also have been a deeply embarrassing fact to have made public. The public might have assumed that marriage to a former glamour girl with a racy past would be a passionate union, and so it was initially. But, by this stage in the relationship, it seemed that the passion was long gone. Yet another sign that there was no going back.

It was also a turning point. Until that detail emerged, there had always seemed the possibility that the two might be able to patch things up: now they couldn't. Not when such intimate details of their lives had become public for all to see and hear. Both were forced to face up to a situation that neither had ever expected, and to make the best of it in the unforgiving glare of the public eye. Rumour and counter-rumour swirled about. Both appeared distraught, yet there seemed to be nothing that either could do about it. Events were gaining a momentum of their own: it seemed that Katie and Pete were by now not so much controlling events as being gripped by them. They were on a rollercoaster, and they couldn't get off.

So, with a whole range of problems in the background, the couple prepared for what lay ahead. And it was a mess. They were angry about money, jealousy, sex, who was to gain custody of the children, who would get the houses (at this early stage in the game, no one was even thinking about the division of the properties) and how they were going to reconcile it with their families. Katie and two of the children were in the Maldives, Pete was in Cyprus and Harvey was at home in the UK. Just what would happen next?

CHAPTER TWO
THE SPLIT DEEPENS

Pete was not after Katie's money, that much was clear. But, despite his assurances that he didn't want her cash, Katie was clearly taking no chances: only days after the separation was announced, she was said to be in talks with Fiona Shackleton, the lawyer hired by Sir Paul McCartney to protect his fortune from ex-wife Heather Mills. For reasons not entirely obvious, Can Associates and Katie were parting company, although they would go on representing Peter. She was becoming distressed at criticism that she had left Harvey at home, and wrote on Twitter, 'Missing Harvey soo much wish he was here but had 2 stay at home for his routine an health an did not want to disrupt that.'

Twitter was playing quite a large part in the unfolding events. Pete had used it, too, after the terrible argument was screened to announce that the row had been resolved within the hour, and that he was not happy the producers had shown it. Again, his pride came to the fore. Some observers even suggested that, had the argument not been screened, the couple would have kissed and made up, as they had done on previous occasions, and that it was only the public nature of the row that brought matters to a head.

'This is the last thing Peter wanted,' said a friend. 'In fact, this is the last thing either of them wanted to happen. They mean a great deal to each other still. But he is a man who has pride and he felt humiliated by what she said. Everybody has their pride. We are all keeping our fingers crossed that they will reconcile, but for the time being the separation is very much real.'

Clearly, the controversy over what was happening with Harvey wasn't helping, either. A friend spoke out to explain what had been going on. 'When the news came out that Peter had called time on the marriage, she just needed to get away,' said the friend. 'She so wanted to take Harvey with her, but knew for medical reasons it was impossible. Harvey needs specialist care and she knew where she was going couldn't provide it. So, with much heartache, she left him in the UK. Katie is really lost without Harvey. She has spoken to him on the phone repeatedly and assured him she will be home soon. She is extremely upset and in tears about being so far away from

Harvey, and it was a decision she didn't take lightly... She is furious he has been left home alone and thought Peter would be there all the time for him.'

Pete was getting drawn into this side of the row, too, and friends spoke out on his behalf. 'For five years, Pete has brought Harvey up as his own flesh and blood,' said one. 'He loves the boy as much as he does his own biological children and the fact Kate has Junior and Princess with her at the moment is killing him. He asked to fly Harvey out to Cyprus with him and had flights provisionally booked. He was told Harvey wasn't allowed any more days off from his special school. But, even when Pete suggested flying him over to Cyprus this weekend, the answer was still, "No".

'Kate told him she wanted Harvey to be with her mother, not him. He is absolutely gutted. The pair had several furious phone calls and some pretty hostile things were said. Frankly, all Pete is thinking of now are the kids. He is speaking to them every single day on the phone and on Skype, but it's not enough. He feels as though he's been banned from seeing his own children.'

Underneath all the mudslinging, a tale of real sadness was beginning to emerge. Any break-up can be hard not only on the parents, but also on the children, and in this case matters were complicated by the fact that, while Harvey was not actually Pete's biological child, he was his son in every other way. Just a few days previously, on the couple's reality show, Pete had spoken about his feelings for Harvey: 'Even though his mum's there, I'm completing the other half,' he said. 'It's complete now. He's changed my life.'

Harvey had also provided inspiration for the new album. 'I've done probably the most special song – it's totally personal – it's all about Harvey,' Pete revealed. 'I always wanted to write something about him, but never knew what to say. Now I'm finally saying it. I hope one day that he'll be able to understand. He'll be able to hear this and know that it's about him.' The song was called 'Unconditional' and the lyrics were certainly touching and the message was clear: Harvey had taught him about the joys of fatherhood even before his own biological children arrived.

'Peter said he had always wanted to write a song about his bond with Harvey and in the end that song became the biggest ballad on his new album,' said a friend. 'He said he wanted to set to music how he felt about the boy and got pretty emotional. He gave a terrific vocal performance on the song for Harvey and said it was because it was so close to his heart. Peter said he was grateful to Harvey for making him a father before he became a biological dad with his own children by Katie.'

And he had been a hands-on father, too. 'He said it meant a lot to him that Harvey calls out "Dad" to him in the night as well as "Mum" if he wakes up crying,' the friend continued. 'He said he wanted to adopt Harvey but hadn't been able to so far for various reasons. He said he found that frustrating and still hoped he could adopt him in the end. Who knows now if that will ever happen or if they will get back together as a couple and as a family?'

But that was looking increasingly unlikely by the day.

Katie continued to keep her fans in touch by posting on Twitter on 19 May: 'Nobody knows anything but us... This is such an awful time for us and I really appreciate all your messages and support. I'm still keeping a dignified silence, I have made no comments, they are made up. I'm heartbroken. I never wanted any of this. We all miss Pete.'

Meanwhile, yet more revelations began to emerge about the stress the marriage had been under, not least because the two of them had wanted to live in different places, Pete in the States and Katie back in the UK.

'Pete loves the way of life in LA and has been enjoying recording his album there,' said a friend. 'He also thinks it's done no end of good for the children. Harvey, in particular, has come on in leaps and bounds in his language development while he's been at school there. Pete wanted the family to set up home there, but Kate really missed the UK. She's very close to her family and missed her mum. She also really missed her horses. She had one flown over to LA and found a riding school, but she didn't like it as much as back home and didn't get to ride as much as she wanted. She said the instructors had very different teaching styles.

'People may scoff but Kate is a very capable and passionate rider and hasn't yet ruled out the Olympics. She would want to be trained in the UK for that.'

Did Katie and Peter have anything in common any more? It was becoming increasingly difficult to tell what that might be, and the full ramifications of that infamous night out were now beginning to show. It emerged that another person in the party that night was Katie's dressage coach, Andrew Gould, although Andrew is married and there was no suggestion the two had been having an affair. Friends were beginning to wonder, though, if Katie was developing feelings for him; he was part of a very different life from the one she had led so far, and it was a sign that her increasing involvement with the horsey set was creating a barrier between herself and Pete; now the two were simply spending their time in different worlds.

'Kate and I, and all her friends, have always socialised at shows and horse events,' said Andrew, when his name first became public, possibly not realising the size of the storm about to break. 'It was all harmless stuff and it has been blown out of proportion. We were just out socialising with friends as we normally would. I don't see it's going to change. She's obviously quite distressed about what's going on. It's a time she needs to be alone with her family, so I will respect that.' Rather unwisely, perhaps, he continued, 'I would say Peter is jealous because we have a close link – as far as horses go. It's just a horse thing.' But,

In June 2009, Katie took a much-publicised holiday to Ibiza to get away from the stresses back in England and let her hair down.

After the breakdown of their marriage was made public, Peter escaped to Cyprus with his brothers Chris and Marcus.

Above: Katie tries to take her mind off her relationship problems by going for a horse ride in Buckinghamshire.

Right: Katie and Princess Tiáamii arrive back from the Maldives, where she fled to avoid media scrutiny.

Peter Andre's first public appearance after the split was at the O2 Arena in London to launch the male burlesque show *Here Come the Boys!*

Katie reappeared in the public eye at the Clothes Show Live in London, where she participated in the UK Beauty Awards beauty pageant as 'Miss London' and promoted her line of equestrian clothing.

Katie's skeletal appearance sparked fears amongst her friends and family that the break-up was taking a drastic toll on her figure.

Three men were rumoured to be involved in their split.

Above: Katie with her dressage coach, Andrew Gould.

Bottom left: Dane Bowers, Katie's ex-boyfriend, with his wife Chrissie Johnston (from whom he recently separated).

Bottom right: Spencer Wilton, the 'mystery man' in the Bristol nightclub photographs.

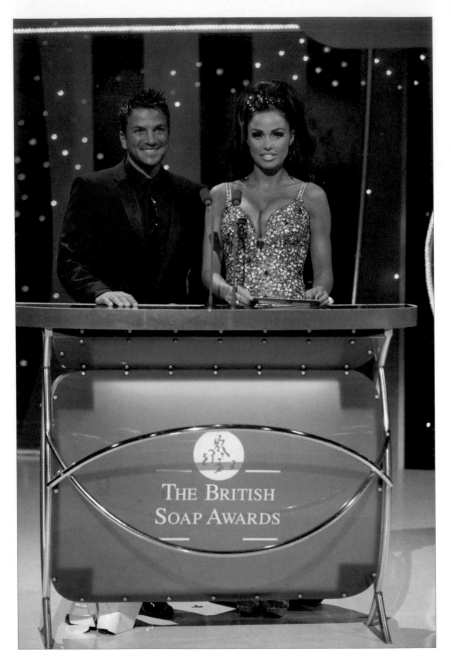

Katie and Peter seemed very happy together at the British Soap Awards, their last public outing before they announced their separation.

if he thought that would be an end to it, he would be proved very wrong.

Pete certainly wasn't thrilled by this new set of friends. 'Peter would try to organise a family day out only to discover that Katie had disappeared with her horsey crowd,' one source close to the couple revealed. 'She moaned about him going out, but it was OK for her to do it. But there was a massive row back in January when Katie was angry at Peter spending a lot of time in the gym when he was trying to lose weight.

'She started going ballistic and accused him of having an affair. They've been bickering really badly for some time. It got to the point where Peter just couldn't put up with it any more and had to get out. But she has known for some time that the marriage is dead. The big problem is her complete obsession with the horsey set and Andrew, and that whole social scene. It has become all-consuming for her, and she seems smitten with Andrew. Suddenly, she's been reinvented from Jordan, the girl with the boobs, to Katie Price. Andrew is well spoken, very middle class and well connected in the equestrian world – and totally different to any man she's met before.'

It was hardly surprising that Pete would feel touchy about any of this. He came from a different world: the Australian-Cypriot upbringing, the pop-star background, plus the aura of showbiz. This is what Katie had seemed to be part of, too, when they first met, but now she was associating with the county set. Had the two not been well known and even if their rows had not been televised, this would have put a strain on any relationship. Certainly, it seemed to be the case with theirs.

It was not long before it emerged that, for some time now, Katie had been making it clear to observers that her marriage had run into severe difficulty. Mona Lewis, who had been a contender on *The Apprentice*, was witness to an astonishing scene a full two months before the split became known to anyone else. The two bumped into one another in the Oceana nightclub in Brighton and it wasn't long before Katie was in full confessional mode.

She was certainly not holding anything back: 'Me and Pete are splitting up... I've fallen for someone else,' she told Mona, before tearing off her wedding ring. 'Have it. It means fuck-all to me.'

Mona couldn't believe what she'd heard. 'Katie said she wanted this new man, but also her family life with Peter Andre,' she related. 'She said her children meant the world to her, but she didn't love Peter and was totally dismissive of him. She started telling me about her marriage and my jaw just dropped; I couldn't believe what I was hearing. I went up to ask her for a photo and next thing she was telling me her marital problems. We're both mums so we started talking about our kids. Then Katie said to me, "I may as well tell you that me and Pete are splitting up." You're going to see it in our TV series, anyway.'

As for that wedding ring – 'It weighed a ton but she

couldn't have cared less about it,' said Mona. 'I could have run off with it there and then. I tried to give it back but she wouldn't take it. I had to grab her hand and practically force it back on her wedding finger.'

When the pair of them went off to the loos, Katie acted more strangely still. 'Lots of girls wanted to speak to her when she went to the loos and there was a crowd of about ten girls around her at the washbasins,' Mona recalled. 'She was wearing a tiny red dress, barely bigger than a T-shirt. Then out of the blue she just stripped off her dress so she was standing in front of us all wearing nothing but a tiny G-string. She was saying, "Look at me. I'm so fat. I'm such a fat c**t. I hate my body. I've been training for the marathon and I'm fat."

'It was crazy. She is absolutely tiny. She has no hips and no bum, but has these enormous boobs. Then she changed tack completely and started ranting about men saying, "They're all fucking bastards. All men are wankers" – doing hand-gestures to illustrate it. She's very expressive when she talks and was waving her arms in the air. The drink she had went flying all down her, but she just carried on going. Lots of girls were asking her for advice about business and she stayed in the loos for nearly an hour talking about her career and how to make money.'

Sadly, it all seemed indicative of a certain degree of self-loathing: why would Katie, rich, beautiful with a successful career, three children and a husband who clearly loved her, whatever the state of the relationship, need to hate herself so much? And it is a question that might be answered by events far back in her past, of which more later.

In the meantime, the rumours about Katie's relationship with Andrew Gould just would not go away. If he had thought his initial words on the subject would put an end to the speculation, he could not have been more wrong: if anything, the story was gathering momentum, and it was now beginning to affect him personally as well. He was, after all, married, and constant speculation that there was something more than friendship and a professional relationship between him and Katie was beginning to take its toll.

Polly Gould, aged 29, Andrew's wife and the mother of his two sons, aged two and four, had naturally taken rather a dim view of reports linking her husband and Katie. She, too, decided to speak out in the hope of putting a stop to all the rumours and insinuation, but, as before, it was a lost cause. The story of the glamour model torn between a pop star and a posh rider was simply too fascinating for people to drop, whatever the truth behind it all.

'I wish we had never got involved with her,' Polly wearily told the *People*. '[But] we chose to go out with her. It was our choice, there is no one else to blame. I am not happy about it at all; I am not happy I got involved in her life, I am not happy that it has come to this. Jordan became a client of my husband and mine too, as we both run a horse business. He teaches her and I look after her horses, and that was supposed to be it. But I am sure there will be other stories to come out and I am cross the focus has shifted on to us like this.'

It was certainly something the couple had never had to face before. They were themselves, perhaps, quite as impressed with Katie as she had been with them, for her world would have no doubt seemed as fascinating to them as theirs was to her. In Katie, they had had an inside look into the world of celebrity, and they clearly found it intriguing. However, they were not prepared for the fallout.

Since the initial reports had come out, stories had been flying about all over the place, including rumours that the Goulds had either split up in the past or were just about to do so. 'We are happily married and I am sure there will be others questioning if that is true,' Polly said. 'But we are happy and strong enough to survive this. I know we chose to go out with her, but I wish people would now just leave us alone. It's unfair of people to make stuff up about our marriage. They are wrong. It is wrong that people say we split up last year. We have never split up over Katie.'

Andrew himself appeared pretty annoyed and spoke out again in another attempt to deflect the attention of the world. 'Katie Price will not break up my marriage,' he said firmly in the *People*. 'I have spoken to Katie, but only about business. She has got four horses that we need to get sorted, but I've left her alone about her private life. People want dirt about us, but Katie will not break up my marriage. Polly and I are fine. It is very difficult being in the middle of a celebrity break-up like this; it's one of the biggest in a while, so it has been very difficult for us. But Polly is cool. She isn't at all worried. She trusts me – she has no reason not to. We've been together for twelve years so this isn't the first time that we have had problems, but it's fine. Katie and Pete have got to sort out their own differences. They have got to decide if they are going to stay together or divorce.'

As her riding instructor, someone in whom she'd clearly confided, he was in a bit of a fix. 'I can't say anything about their split because it will just fuel things even more,' said Andrew, who was rapidly learning that not all publicity is good publicity. 'Me and Polly have never split up over Katie: we are all friends and we work together. She would come round if we were about to go out on to a function. The last time I spoke to Katie was two days ago and that was about horses; since then, there has been no contact. Katie owes me for all of this. All I did was go out for a drink with her and now this has been blown out of all proportion. When we went to the club, I was there, we all just went for dinner and then for a drink. It was just kids with mobile phones who were taking the pictures.'

Indeed, he was beginning to sound thoroughly

exasperated. Would Katie deny there had been an affair? 'Katie will do what Katie wants to do,' he said wearily. 'She won't listen to a word that I say; she'll do what she wants. There were no plans for her to break up, it just happened very quickly. There was no reason for Pete to be jealous. I did say I wasn't the guy in the club. I didn't mind it coming out, but Kate didn't want Pete to know I was there because of how he reacts. I don't know why he has that problem, but I have to respect Kate's choice.'

They had certainly been friends. Paul Crutchley, landlord of the Bolney Stage pub, a local haunt of the horsey set, had seen them in there from time to time. 'I know Andrew Gould and Katie Price, and, yes, she has come in here with her friends from the riding stables and, yes, she has been here with him,' he said. 'They always come in for luncheon and she has never flashed her boobs here like she did at the nightclub. She was much more discreet.'

As if all this were not enough, there was now widespread speculation that the duo split as a publicity stunt. Pete had finally had enough – he had said very little in public, but now he was prompted to speak out. 'How anyone could think I would pretend to split up from my wife to grab headlines is beyond me,' he said. 'I can assure you it's not; it's just sick. Katie and I have separated and it has been a totally devastating week for me, to say the least. I'm crushed. I don't really want to go into any detail as it's all still so raw... I'm completely crushed.'

Pete ate regularly at a nearby establishment in Cyprus, Viale, and a member of staff there, Katarina Mavromati, expressed her concern. 'He is very sad and just picks at his food now,' she said. 'He pushes it around the plate; he is too upset to eat. He's been coming here for years with Katie and his children. I am worried about him.'

And she wasn't alone. His uncle, Michael Violaris, had also been trying to help. 'Peter is very confused,' he said. 'I cannot get exactly inside his mind, but all day long he sits around the house with all these thoughts going through his mind. He's got his head in his hands, thinking. The family have been telling him to get back together with Katie, to go back to how things used to be. We want them to get back together. Peter's trying to understand what to do.'

By now, unsurprisingly, the couple's celebrity friends were beginning to speak out, with one, Ulrika Jonsson, denying the rumours that the split was a publicity stunt. 'Not unlike me, she chose from a conveyor belt of unsuitable men with whom she was unable to sustain suitable decent relationships,' she said. 'In my opinion – indeed, in my experience – these two people do truly love each other. I don't believe this is some vulgar publicity stunt engineered to further bloat their £30 million empire.'

Another person to comment publicly on the couple's estrangement was Mel B, although, if truth be told, she was not so much a mutual friend as one of Pete's exes – the couple had dated over a decade earlier. 'Please take Katie back,' the ex-Spice Girl said. 'Pete's a great guy – it's a really sad situation. Pete and Katie are really popular in LA, and so I hope they get back together – especially as there are kids involved. We have all made mistakes. I know my husband Stephen has done some crazy things in the past but I love him like mad, and he loves me. Pete should give Katie a second chance. Everyone deserves one. [They are] fantastic, lovely people. From what I know, they are madly in love – and love conquers all.'

Some observers felt that Mel's intervention might actually have done more harm than good, not least because, at the time she and Pete had been an item, he had referred to her as 'the one'. Katie had spoken about it publicly, too: 'He admits she got him wrapped around her little finger, which is far too much information for me. Pete has been with so many girls and I hate it. I'll never trust him 100 per cent. It's what we've argued about most.'

Once more, Andrew Gould also tried to distance himself from everything that was going on. Yet again he was forced to say there was 'nothing going on' between himself and Katie. He said, to prove it, he wanted to have a word with Pete, man to man. 'All this fuss over one drink I had with Kate,' he said. 'I've had drinks with lots of my clients, but, because she is famous, this has been turned into something it's not. I haven't spoken to Peter. I have spoken to Kate, but that's my duty: to tell her how her horses are doing. I think Kate needs to sit down and talk with Peter.

They need to sit down and properly talk things over. Meet me man to man... and I'll save your marriage.'

But it was all too late. According to Katie herself, it really was over now: 'I love my husband, but I can't sit around crying,' she revealed to *OK!* magazine. 'This is a new chapter in my life. Pete can't blame this on the drinking. Over the five years of our relationship, I've probably been out twenty times. I'm not a party girl and I don't drink at home so, when I go out, I can get drunk quickly.' Again, this bore all the hallmarks of a row that had erupted over and over again throughout the years.

Nor did anyone expect Katie Price to sit around crying. In the past, she had coped with some momentous problems, not least being left by Dwight Yorke while she was pregnant with their son and then going on to discover that Harvey suffered from disabilities. There was no question that, sad as it was, she would be able to cope with this.

'Katie is a feisty, independent woman who has taken a lot of emotional knocks in her life,' said a friend. 'She has dusted herself down before and got on with living; she is ready to do it again. It's just a shame Pete didn't want to stay for the journey.'

Well, that was one way of putting it – Pete himself seemed hardly thrilled by recent events. But battle lines were being drawn now and, given that the chance of a reconciliation seemed increasingly slim, naturally both parties would have to work out their next move. Matters were becoming heated and clearly this ongoing rumour and counter-rumour mill could not be allowed to proceed, running totally out of control.

By late May, the couple had both returned to the UK: Katie headed for the former marital home, while Pete went to stay at the home of Claire Powell, who had previously managed both of them, but now worked only for him.

It didn't look as if it would, in any way, be an amicable split. On returning to Britain, almost the first thing both of them did was to consult their lawyers. It was rumoured that Pete would fight for full access to both his children (although not Harvey): he was unlikely to be successful in this, but, tactically, it meant he might get joint custody.

'He is devastated at what is happening, but he knows if a divorce goes ahead, Katie will fight tooth and nail for everything,' revealed a friend to the *Sun*. 'He loves his kids and the idea he might have limited access is breaking his heart.'

It was certainly the children, not the money, that was Pete's priority. As he made his way to his lawyers, Clintons, it emerged this was actually his second meeting with them – the first had been held before the couple announced they would part. 'Forget money: all I care about are my kids,' he told them as they began to hash out exactly how he could play a role in all the children's lives, including Harvey's. Clearly, he couldn't go for full custody there, but he had been Harvey's father for years and wanted to maintain a good relationship with him, much as he did Junior and Princess.

'Pete has no interest in discussing his financial rights,' said a friend to the *Mirror*. 'His sole priority is his children and Harvey. Both Kate and Pete want the divorce to be amicable, but it is still very early days and things have already turned far nastier than anyone could have ever predicted. Pete's a great dad and wants regular access to his kids, which means joint custody. He is praying Kate appreciates this and doesn't block the move. It is so rare for a father to be granted sole custody, but, if Kate was to go off the rails, then clearly this is what he would push for. It's not about the money – he doesn't want to profit from divorce. He'll come out only with what he put into their three-and-a-half-year marriage, but it is still an incredibly messy situation and deeply unpleasant.'

By mid-June, the stress was getting to Katie and she set off for a week's holiday in Ibiza. It was to hit the headlines for all the wrong reasons and lead some people to question whether, as a good mother, which she had always been, she should be behaving in such an openly hedonistic way. In retrospect, her behaviour was clearly a sign of how much the split had devastated her, but at the time it raised eyebrows back home.

It was Pete who looked after the children when Katie went away, taking all three of them back to Cyprus with him, while his estranged wife headed for the bars and the beach.

Katie arrived at the Es Vive hotel – one of the trendiest on the island and out of bounds to children – with seven friends and the film crew for her new reality-TV series. She had started as she meant to go on by drinking champagne on the plane and, when the group arrived at the hotel, they headed straight to the pool and ordered a jug of sangria.

'Yee haa, I'm going to have some fun at last,' Katie told friends. 'It's been a fucking nightmare but I'm going to have a wicked time. I haven't had a full week's holiday for ten years. I am well up for it.'

And so it was to prove. For the time being, however, a friend explained to the *Daily Mirror* why Katie wanted to get away. 'Katie feels absolutely drained,' she said. 'She's had an emotionally knackering five weeks and wants to let her hair down. Kate believes she works bloody hard for her money and deserves this trip. She's not got the kids with her so she's not tied down. If she wants to go out every night and get hammered, then why shouldn't she? After all, she's a single lady now.'

Unfortunately, it didn't take long for matters to spiral out of control. Given the stress that she'd been under, and the fact that she'd lost a lot of weight, Katie was not in the best state to deal with the amount of alcohol she was consuming. She and her friends spent the day drinking, and then headed off to Eden Nightclub in San Antonio, where a nasty fracas ensued with a member of the public.

When she got into the nightclub, the group continued drinking, and Katie was pictured snogging Anthony Lowther, a 28-year old model, as well as an ex-boyfriend, Matt Peacock. She was also dancing very suggestively. 'It was pretty steamy stuff,' an onlooker told the *Daily Star*. 'She kept hitching her dress up and didn't seem to care that we could all see everything. She was grinding up against the lads and her girlfriends and their hands were all over her.'

It was to go downhill from there.

Anthony was to become something of a fixture that week. The next night, after Katie had spent the day posing on a speedboat for her calendar, the group had drinks at the hotel, before heading off to Angelo, a gay restaurant. Anthony was enjoying himself, telling the *Mirror* she was 'better off without Pete'.

'I'm having a great time with Katie,' he continued. 'She's getting on with her life and enjoying herself without Pete. I know her from a few photoshoot jobs I've done with her and we've always got on. She's having a blast and is enjoying being single again.'

That was more than could be said for Pete. Over in Cyprus, he was seen weeping in the arms of his mother, and, given the pictures of his estranged wife that were now being flashed around the world, that was hardly surprising.

Meanwhile, Katie was becoming the subject of criticism

back home, with people asking, 'What is a mother-of-three doing, behaving like this?'

But Katie was unrepentant. 'It's his own doing,' she said. 'He's bleating to his mum. He wanted this divorce, he instigated it, and he got what he wanted. So why is he upset? He's crying. That's normal, he's emotional.'

Pete was increasingly distressed. 'It's like a wild animal has been unleashed,' he was reported as saying in the *Sunday Mirror*. 'I don't recognise her as my wife. Has she no idea what this will be like for the kids? It was Katie who I fell in love with and married. But it looks like she just wanted all along to be her old self, Jordan. I can't believe what I'm seeing. She's like a caged animal that's been let out.'

Other people couldn't believe it either. Katie was posing in a series of increasingly provocative outfits, including a gold-lamé number comprising hot pants and a cutaway top. It was extremely revealing. She had scratched over a tattoo of Pete on her wrist, leading to speculation that she'd had it removed.

By now, there was also something of a backlash on the island, and, when she and Anthony turned up in the Boho club, a group of young men managed to gatecrash the VIP area and started chanting, 'We love Pete.' For a short time, it looked as if matters might be getting out of hand.

Anthony was not used to this kind of behaviour, and he was beginning to sound a bit unnerved. 'We're having great time together. I really love her, she's a very sexy girl,' he said. 'Everyone's saying we're boyfriend and girlfriend but we're just having a bit of fun. It's been a wild few days and all the attention has been quite scary at times.'

Over in Cyprus, Pete's mother was rushed to hospital, while he continued to care for Harvey, Junior and Princess. And it must be said, he was being pretty magnanimous. 'I still love Kate,' he wrote in *New* magazine. 'If you get over someone in five weeks, you obviously didn't love them in the first place. I know everyone is waiting for me to comment on all the stories in the papers but I can't read any of them. I know it will only cause me pain. I just don't want to put myself through it. There are only three people in the world that are my priority and that's the kids.'

Pete was certainly winning the sympathy vote, while, back in Ibiza, the partying continued, with Katie now wearing a see-through baby-doll dress as she and Anthony hit the clubs once more.

As the week began to draw to an end, Katie had clearly begun to realise how her behaviour was playing back home. She didn't help her own cause, though, in the way in which she attempted to point out that it was Pete who had left, not her. 'Loving Ibiza can't wait to see my children where there [sic] back from Cyprus!' she wrote on her Twitter page. 'Pete being a true c**t to me! He left me nt me leave him. [sic]'

Her mother Amy was certainly aware of how this

appeared to the outside world. The *People* reported she said to Katie. 'Can't you see what you are doing to your family? Going out night after night doesn't exactly set the right example. How do you think it looks on the outside?'

But Katie's last night on the island went much as before. She and her friends lurched between their rooms and the bar, banging on the doors of people's rooms, before she chanted, 'We are staying another night, we are staying another night in Ibiza.'

And with that it was back to Blighty, where she appeared in relatively demure garb at the airport, a cardigan and jeans. A couple of days later she was pictured out riding again. It had been an unfortunate episode – and sadly not one that hinted at an amicable resolution to the divorce.

This was certainly not what had been expected when the two staged their spectacular wedding just a few years previously, let alone when that fateful meeting in the celebrity jungle took place. For a while, it had seemed as if Katie and Pete really were the gilded couple: the stars who met on reality TV and whose romance had been played out in front of millions of viewers. They had fascinated and enthralled the nation, kept everyone on their toes at every twist and turn in their lives and in many ways seemed to be living the dream. The birth of their children only seemed to reinforce that here was a couple of the moment, a pair who seemed to sum up everything about early-21st-century life. Apart, they were already famous; together, they had seemed virtually unstoppable. So just why, from that first encounter in the celebrity jungle, had it all gone so badly wrong?

CHAPTER THREE
JANUARY

The rumour mill had gone into overdrive. It was January 2004, and one of the most popular programmes on television, *I'm A Celebrity... Get Me Out Of Here!* was returning to the screens for its third series. The line-up of celebrities due to appear was being finalised. Among them was a 25-year-old glamour model, then known as Jordan, who had become famous for her remarkable surgically enhanced figure, and who had left a series of famous boyfriends in her wake.

Then a single mother-of-one, Jordan, whose fame seemed to be waning a bit at the time, was said to be demanding (and getting) £100,000 for her appearance, twice the usual rate of the other contestants, with a great deal of speculation as to how she was going to survive the tropical heat. She had a boyfriend at the time,

Scott Sullivan; however, the relationship was not destined to last.

It was a curious line-up that year. The other celebrities heading for a spell in the jungle included convicted fraudster Lord Brocket, ex-Sex Pistol John Lydon, Alex Best, the estranged wife of George Best, former Atomic Kitten Kerry Katona, athlete Diane Modahl, ex-footballer Neil 'Razor' Ruddock, DJ Mike Read, and the former BBC royal correspondent Jennie Bond. Oh, and one other name had come up: Peter Andre, a musician of Cypriot descent, who was born in Harrow, England, and brought up in Australia. He had had some success as a singer back in the 1990s after being discovered on the Australian TV talent show *New Faces* in 1990, but his star had been on the wane for some time now and not much attention was paid to his inclusion in the show.

Not so Jordan. From the moment her involvement was announced – through her appearance with her hair specially plaited in dreadlocks (a very good way of keeping it under control in the sticky conditions that lay ahead), sporting a bright-pink fluffy jacket as she made her way through Heathrow to board the plane that would take her to the other side of the world – the world, in turn, was intrigued as to what lay ahead. No one was to be disappointed, although what would transpire in the jungle over the next few weeks was certainly not what anyone had anticipated. After dating a succession of men who had let her down or disappointed her, finally Jordan was to find love. The creepy crawlies she would have to put up with in return were a small price to pay.

But at the time, no one, least of all Jordan, had a clue what would happen next. Attention was focusing on possible rivalry between her and Kerry Katona, on the grounds that both of them had large chests, while Jordan herself was in no doubt as to what was expected of her on the television screen. 'I know it'll be really hot,' she asserted confidently. 'I won't be self-conscious getting my kit off. If there's a good sunbathing spot, I'll strip off so I don't get any white lines. I'll be getting everything out. I'll be in my birthday suit.' But then she added, 'If there was someone I fancied in the jungle, well, you never know...'

Those words were to prove more prophetic than she could possibly have imagined.

Even before they actually met, Peter and Jordan were expressing an interest in each other. 'I'd be a very lucky man if Jordan pounced on me,' said Peter, who at the time was living in Cyprus, in an interview shortly before the programme began. 'I've never met her, but I've seen pictures and she's extremely attractive. I came to England yesterday and she was all over the papers. She seems really nice.'

The attraction, it seemed, was mutual. 'When I was younger, I really fancied Peter,' revealed Jordan. 'I thought he was gorgeous.'

Anyone who thought Jordan would not be able to cope with the ordeal that lay ahead did not know the woman. That she could give as good as she got was more than apparent in an interview she gave when she arrived in Australia: posing with a 9ft python, she asserted, 'I quite enjoyed having a snake slithering over my boobs and I've had worse things on me – I've slept with Dane Bowers. I work around horses a lot, so I'm used to rats, too. And nothing in that jungle could be a bigger rat than my son Harvey's father, Dwight Yorke.'

And then came another prophetic remark. 'The only thing Scott's said I can't do is sleep with Peter Andre,' she continued. 'He said I can sling my hook if I do as I will have brought shame on myself for bedding a man who has that bad a haircut.'

All the contestants stayed at the six-star Versace hotel before the show eventually began. After initial introductions, insiders noted a spark between Jordan and Peter straight away. But he had competition, not least from Lord Brocket, who at one stage was photographed having wedged a champagne glass in Jordan's cleavage. However, Peter was determined to get in her good books right away: at a training session before the celebrities entered the jungle, he was flirting wildly with her, before lying down and putting his head in her lap. 'Whenever Jordan was around, Peter would be by her side,' remarked one observer. 'He looked like a lovesick fifteen-year-old boy.'

And that was before they set foot in the jungle itself.

The entrance to the jungle was made by helicopter: Jordan and Neil were the first to endure the now infamous Bushtucker Trial, donning helmets into which all sorts of unpleasant insects were poured. Somehow they got through it. Afterwards, Jordan, then still best known as a topless model, peeled off most of her outerwear to get rid of all the insects, leaving only a bra, G-string and boots. 'I can't believe I just did that,' she declared. 'I am up for any challenge now!'

More pertinently, perhaps, Jordan appeared to dump Scott live on air. 'I'm not happy with my boyfriend,' she told the other celebrities present. 'He's not my boyfriend as far as I'm concerned at the minute. He hasn't wished me luck, hasn't texted me for two/three days. Nothing.'

But it seemed his replacement was waiting in the wings. Even at that early stage, Kerry was telling Jordan she thought Peter was in love with the glamour model and, of course, she was right.

As John Lydon undertook the next trial – being assaulted by ostriches – the relationship between Jordan and Peter was already beginning to hot up. The two were seen discussing her breast implants, before Peter told her he loved her and gave her a hug. At that stage, Jordan did not allow matters to progress further, but nor did she look displeased.

However, John Lydon was another matter altogether,

singularly failing to be won over by her charms, and at one memorable point telling her, 'Take your implants out of my face!'

But Jordan didn't appear to care. Peter was clearly becoming enamoured of Katie and she was forming a bond with Kerry, so what was there for her to worry about?

And on top of that, back in the UK, public perception of her was beginning to change. Famous as she had been, until that series of *I'm A Celebrity...*, Jordan was primarily a glamour model with a male fan base. Now women were beginning to warm to her, too. She had received a lot of sympathy after Dwight Yorke left her in late 2001 when she became pregnant and went on to have a disabled child, Harvey. Now she was demonstrating again that she was a woman with plenty of guts. She endured the Bushtucker Trials with a lot of grace and good humour – and, indeed, bravery – which played very well on the TV screens. But she gave Neil Ruddock all the credit for surviving the trials themselves. 'I didn't think I'd do it, but I knew I had to,' she said. 'I wasn't calm. I think I survived because I was holding his hand.'

And, of course, there was that budding romance with Peter. It certainly wasn't doing her prospects any harm. The odds on her winning the show were slashed from 7/1 to 3/1: in the event, it wasn't to happen, but this was a sign of how she was moving into a whole new league. This was the moment when Jordan moved from being Jordan in the public eye into her real persona – Katie Price. She insisted all her fellow celebrities use the name, and the public were beginning to get used to it, too.

Peter was also being called upon to prove his mettle: having confessed that he was terrified of snakes and spiders, he was forced to stick his head into eight boxes containing Huntsman spiders, pythons and all manner of nasties to dislodge a star using only his teeth. But he did so, winning meals for all ten contestants on the show and showing that he, too, was brave and a good sport, thereby winning audience approval. And, by now, it was apparent that he really did fancy Jordan: this was not being put on for the cameras.

It was Kerry who teased it out of him. 'You can see you're physically attracted to her,' she said. 'You definitely want a piece of cake, you do! Come on, be a man and admit it. Who wouldn't? Kate's a woman. All women play. You're only human. Fucking hell, I'm female and I want a part of her!'

He did not disagree.

Back in the UK, the people who had known Jordan for years were delighted about the way her image was changing before their very eyes. 'People thought she was just a blonde bimbo with big tits,' said photographer Jeany Savage, who had worked with her for years. 'She is not just a pair of big boobs. She has a brain and it won't surprise me if she goes on to win the show. She doesn't care what people think about her and she is a very driven woman. Basically, she is Katie and her job is Jordan. She will end up winning everyone over. She makes for brilliant viewing and is the star of the show already. When I first knew her, she was pretty gobby, but then she went through a stage of being pretty unsure about herself. Now she is confident again and knows exactly where she's going. I always said to her she was going to be a star! I think the getting drunk and getting in and out of limos was all part of becoming what she is: a young woman.'

Of course, Katie/Jordan had suffered along the way, but that, too, had helped make her stronger. The birth of Harvey in May 2002 and the subsequent discovery of his disabilities had brought her up short, but she had fought back against the circumstances, growing up along the way. 'Having a baby has had a profound effect on her,' revealed Jeany. 'At first, when she was pregnant, she thought, So what? Now Harvey is here and lovely, it's very different. She created Jordan, and she's lived as Jordan for a while, but becoming a mother sent her back to being Katie. What she needs now is a good man but I don't think it'll be Peter Andre. At first I thought they'd make a good-looking couple, but I think he is far too precious.' Of course, this was the only way in which Jeany was wrong.

Jordan's agent Dave Read was equally pleased with the way it was going. 'People are used to seeing her in a nightclub with a drink in her hand,' he said. 'Now they know she's quite down-to-earth. She is a mother and a human being. She is nice, after all! I just wanted people to see the other side of her so she has already achieved, in a couple of days, what I wanted from the whole thing. I can tell from her face she is absolutely revelling in this. She is doing what she wanted – having the trip of a lifetime, earning some money as a single mum and seeing money from the calls going to charity. Although criticism is like water off a duck's back, it might seem a little alien to come out and find people are writing nice things about her.'

Now the flirting between Jordan and Peter was so intense it was steaming up the TV screen, but in retrospect it's possible to spot the problems that lay ahead, even before they'd actually got together. In a nutshell, Peter was becoming very drawn to Katie, but not to Jordan.

'You know the wild side of you that everyone knows?' he said.

'I have got it in me, but I haven't got the energy over here,' Jordan replied.

'I like you better when you're not like that,' said Peter.

'You haven't seen me when I'm like that,' snapped Jordan.

It was a small exchange – but it summed up exactly what was to tear them apart at the end.

The rest of the time, though, they could not have been getting on better. After all, Peter was a singer and had taken to serenading Jordan, singing 'Ain't No Sunshine' to her at one point.

Jordan was also showing a wicked sense of humour.

'I have to feel something to feel something – you know what I mean?' Peter asked her.

A moment passed. 'He's not a tit man is what he's saying,' Jordan replied.

TV bosses then introduced alcohol into the jungle, which lessened the couple's inhibitions still further, and they lay, legs entwined, in a hammock talking about sex.

'I'm not noisy at all,' said Jordan. 'But I reckon you are. I'm a storyteller: I like to tell stories.'

All this was clearly getting Peter into quite a state. 'My whole body is in a state of shock at the moment,' he told the others. 'We've got Jungle Fever.'

It was Alex Best's 32nd birthday that day and the duo got dressed up to celebrate.

'I want you to sex me up,' Peter said to Jordan. 'Make me look like Tarzan to your Jane.'

Matters soon went further still: infrared cameras were in the camp, which meant Peter was caught climbing into Jordan's bed that night. The mosquitoes were bothering them, so they moved to her sleeping bag, where, after a bit of fumbling, Peter began kissing Jordan's neck. In the nick of time, she remembered the cameras and told him he'd better leave; he did, but matters were clearly becoming a little full-on.

The next morning, Jordan appeared to be regretting the night before. 'My fourth night was a disaster,' she said. 'It gets worse by the day. I woke up and you obviously saw Peter come into bed. I was knackered. I was lying there and thought things were not right, so I said, "You had better go – I have to stay away." I don't know... He's a really nice guy, but I have a boyfriend and that's that.' She was obviously very torn – and this was still only day four.

It was all perfect fodder for the viewing public, and John Lydon, whose reaction to Jordan couldn't have been more different to Peter's, provided a perfect foil. While Peter was by now pretty much wandering around with his tongue hanging out, John was getting increasingly irascible about his pneumatic companion, and matters came to a head when he felt Jordan had failed to put any logs on the campfire.

'Some people don't do nothing at all and one person in particular,' he said meaningfully. 'Whatever career that thing thinks she has, it's a pretty useless one in my opinion. Hello? Jordan? When are you actually going to do something? If that girl lifts a finger, it's only to do her nails. God, moany old bitch! She's so spoiled she gets on my tits. I can't stand her, I'll be honest. I've done enough, I think, I've done enough for me.'

Jordan, not surprisingly, was unmoved. 'I don't give a shit what he thinks! I'm here to do my bit,' she retorted. 'I may not be as quick off the mark as other people, but at least I do my bit.'

Anyway, why should she care what he thought? Peter

was mooning around like a love-struck teen and the viewing public were loving her. One curmudgeonly old Sex Pistol wasn't going to change that.

But still, Jordan seemed a little torn. As Peter confessed his feelings for her to Kerry, she was seen to move a diamond ring to her engagement finger, a gesture some people interpreted as a show of loyalty to Scott. Others thought she might be toying with him, including Jordan's mother Amy, who was also out in Australia, looking after Harvey and watching her daughter on screen. 'She is probably teasing him, knowing he won't get anywhere,' she said in a *GMTV* interview.

As for Jordan herself, who could blame her for being a little wary? Not only had she had her own much-publicised man troubles in the past, but she was also slightly concerned about Pete's motives. 'I read that he was going to try it on with me anyway,' she told Kerry, worrying that Peter really wanted her in order to raise his own profile. She was wrong, but she wouldn't have been human not to have doubts.

It was John's birthday, and a Mad Hatter's Tea Party and group production of *Oliver!* were staged in his honour after he made an abortive attempt to escape. But he couldn't resist having a go at Jordan again. 'I just don't like lazy people, I don't like carrying dead weight,' he said. 'I don't. That's coming across now really, really strongly. It's a good-for-nothing waste of time at the moment. Make her get up and do something, give her a poke up the arse like she deserves! It's not right – she's dragging it all down to silliness. Much more of that and I'm walking, I'm telling you. I'm not here to support that kind of crap, I'm here to have a laugh with some good people. She can't even bloody wash a teacup without the effort of it all. And it eats and it's non-stop, and it don't cook bugger all!' For good measure, he labelled her a 'page-three blow-up balloon', but Jordan clearly couldn't have cared less.

The viewing figures for that season's *I'm A Celebrity...* were phenomenal: 11 million by then and a huge amount of that was clearly down to Jordan and her growing romance with Peter. John, with his bad-tempered outbursts, was doing his own bit, while some of the others – most notably Lord Brocket, who clearly appreciated the female company around him, Kerry and Jennie Bond – were also attracting a fair bit of attention, but it was Jordan, as the rest of the nation still called her, who was really the big draw.

Someone else who was delighted that Jordan's image was changing was her stepfather, Paul Price. Married to Jordan's mother Amy for fifteen years at that stage, and with her for 21, Paul had brought Katie up since the age of four and regarded her as his own. Her biological father, Ray Infield, played little part in her life, while Paul and Amy had another daughter, Sophie. The Kate that Paul knew was quite different from the Jordan who had become famous, and so he was pleased the balance was at last being redressed.

'Millions of blokes ogle my daughter's breasts, she's a sex object,' he said to the *Sunday Mirror*. 'But, to me, she will always be little adorable Kate. Of course, it's strange to have men leering at her. It's a weird feeling. People wind me up in the pub, when all I want is to have a quiet drink. It really annoys me when they find out who I am and start making jibes about her breasts. I could punch every guy who slags her off or says crude things about her, but life's too short. I just walk away. She's so different when I'm with her, when she's my little Kate, that it's easy to forget about what she does for a living.'

What was also coming to light was that, although Jordan had made her name falling out of nightclubs, in reality her life was a very different one.

'Kate's a real country girl, and a real family girl too,' continued Paul. 'She comes over to visit all the time. She loves her horses – she spends any spare minute on her horse, going for huge rides over the countryside. And she likes walking too, we all do – nice long walks. She loves it here because she doesn't get any hassle; everyone in the village knows her and treats her as my daughter, not a celebrity.'

It seemed Jordan also got on well with the other women in her family, too. 'Kate's very close to her little sister Sophie and often pops in to see how she's doing,'

Paul continued. 'Her and her mum are close, too – they're like two peas in a pod. Both feisty, go-getting girls, that's what I love about them. Kate leaves Jordan in the studio or the nightclub and comes home as herself, the sweet little girl she's always been. She goes out a lot, but that's her job. She gets paid to stand in a nightclub and look good. But, if she's got a night off, she just likes to curl up on the sofa, cuddle up to Scott and Harvey, and watch a bit of telly. Soaps, reality shows – whatever's on, really. Scott sometimes drags her out because he feels he doesn't go out with her as Kate very often, but really she'd rather be at home.'

This image of a down-to-earth girl, happy to curl up in front of the TV and obsessed with her horses, was a very different one from anything the British public had been exposed to before... and they liked it. Debates were beginning to appear in the papers about whether Jordan was a glamour girl or a feminist icon: the fact that she was an accomplished horsewoman clearly shocked some people. But she was, and that was the persona that was now coming across on television, and the one that Peter was falling for. Indeed, Jordan's transformation was becoming the subject of hot debate, in the broadsheets as well as the tabloids.

Paul was aware of this. 'I think people are seeing that side of her now on *I'm A Celebrity*... and I'm really pleased,' he said. 'That's the girl we know and love – and I'm thrilled everybody else seems to like her, too.' But even he didn't realise that now things were becoming serious with Peter. 'She's just playing a game,' he continued. 'She's trying to wind Scott up. Peter seems a nice enough lad, and in another world maybe they would make a good couple, but Kate would never cheat on Scott. She's a very faithful, loyal girl. She's not going to dump Scott, either – she'll be back in his arms as soon as she gets out.'

However, Paul didn't see a long-term future there, either. 'Scott's a nice enough lad, but he's definitely not the one,' he revealed. 'He's too much of a playboy – he's always on holiday, messing about. He's too young and he's not ready to settle down. Kate's got baby Harvey to think about, she needs some stability in her life – but she's not going to get it from him. Me and Kate's mum have both dropped hints, but Kate's her own woman.' That much was becoming increasingly clear.

Back in the jungle, Jordan created a sensation when she and Peter managed to avoid the cameras and snuck off to canoodle. Until then, it had been assumed that Peter was the keen one, while Jordan was holding back, but now all that was beginning to change. She was showing distinct signs of becoming rather enamoured herself, and, when Peter told her that evening he wasn't 'going to do the beg thing', she even looked a little taken aback. It was the first sign that the two really might have a future once the show came to an end.

The first person to be booted out of the show was Radio DJ Mike Read. Given the dominance of the other personalities, it was hardly surprising. Far more attention was paid to what was going on between Jordan and Peter and now it was clear that it really was becoming serious.

'OK, let me first clear one thing up,' said Peter, in an on-screen heart-to-heart. 'Later, when all this is over, and you've done what you've done, give us a call, all right? That's all I'm going to say.'

Later in the day, Jordan told him, 'I'm doing what you are: if you're backing off, I'm backing off.'

'You were never on,' said Peter.

'Oh, I was,' was her reply.

Clearly, matters were becoming more serious still.

Out in the real world, there were rumours that, incensed by the on-screen flirting with Peter, Scott had dumped her. By then, it was shutting the stable doors long after the horse had bolted, found a new companion and was making a new life for itself in fields, far away.

Scott, however, who had been in the US, until then unaware of what was happening back home, clearly didn't realise that it was all far too late. 'I'm furious that Peter Andre is being disrespectful towards me,' he said. 'He knows Katie is not single and has a boyfriend, but he's still trying it on with her. I'm going to be on the next plane out to Australia and I'm going to punch his lights out. I've been in America for the past few days, so I haven't seen the show but all my friends and family have told me what's been going on and I'm not happy.'

In the jungle, however, Jordan and Peter were having an increasingly difficult time holding back. Everything they did, after all, was caught on camera, and both had the sense to know that there was a line over which they mustn't step. But it wasn't easy. Yet another longing exchange went as follows:

'If I like someone, it's full-on,' said Jordan. 'I'm an all-or-nothing girl.'

'What do you want?' asked Peter.

'You,' was her reply.

'So, does Scott know you're feeling a bit unsure?' asked Peter. (Well, he certainly did now!)

'I know he's not the one,' said Jordan. 'He's a nice guy, but no way! I'm not going to marry him, so why waste my time? Is that deep? Is that bad?'

Peter was clearly desperate for matters to take a step forward physically, but Jordan was being more cautious.

'Not yet,' she warned.

'There has to be one night while we're here when we can just cuddle – sleep and cuddle,' said Peter. 'What's wrong with that? There's no harm in that. I have to just hold you one night.'

'How nice would that be, snuggling up at night?' sighed Jordan wistfully, before sounding a little more circumspect. 'How do I know it's not a game with you?'

'I'm not going to deny I like you,' admitted Peter. 'Why should I deny that? You've told me you feel the same so I reckon that's beautiful, there's nothing wrong with that. I'm just worried if we stay longer, we're just getting closer and closer to it. We came within a millimetre of it.'

They did – but they also managed to take a step back. Both were trying to keep a lid on things until they could finally be alone.

Meanwhile, Commonwealth athlete Diane Modahl was voted out, followed by former Liverpool defender Neil 'Razor' Ruddock, events totally overshadowed by the fact that Jordan and Peter shared their first kiss on screen. The occasion was a treat donated by Irish pop singer Ronan Keating: 'Keating's A Potent Blend' – a chest filled with enough coffee, whiskey and cream for the remaining members of the camp to enjoy Irish coffees. The other campers exchanged exuberant kisses on the cheek, while Peter and Jordan went one further and aimed for the mouth. Then there was another of those longing discussions, this time talking about the fact that Peter had gone over to Jordan's bed and put his head under the covers.

'Was it a good surprise?' asked Peter.

'You did wake me up, actually,' said Jordan.

'That's not what I said. I said, was it a good surprise?' he repeated.

'Yes, it was,' she admitted. 'And the other thing... They won't have seen under there.'

'No, I know,' said Peter.

'I could always say we were whispering,' breathed Jordan.

'I couldn't help myself,' said Peter. And so it went on.

There was a brief diversion from the increasingly amorous couple when John Lydon, having provoked a storm of protest over the use of strong language on the show, walked off. He'd already threatened to do so twice before, but, for whatever the reason, decided he'd had enough and left the show. His departure meant there would be no eviction that night (pundits were divided between those who thought he'd walked because he feared he might lose and those who were of the view that he'd gone because he feared he might win). Whatever the truth, he was out, depriving the show of one of its biggest characters. However, the attention was still very much on the loved-up Jordan and Peter. The press had moved on from questioning whether Jordan was a feminist icon to whether relationships could survive reality TV: no one seemed able to agree. But perhaps they should have realised that a relationship born in front of the cameras risked dying in front of them too. Meanwhile, the duo had the nation hooked on their antics and everyone had a view on what was to come. Now the celebrity jungle was more popular than ever before.

CHAPTER FOUR
JUNGLE FEVER

With John Lydon gone, much to the dismay of some of the viewers, attention really was now focused on Peter and Jordan, as never before. Kerry, Lord Brocket and Jennie Bond were still providing good value, especially when the latter two clashed over what he saw as her obsession with his moneyed background, but the human-interest story unfolding in front of millions of viewers' eyes was just too fascinating for the others to get much of a look-in. But again, there was another small warning to come, when Jordan and Peter had their first row. And what was it about? Another man.

It all began when Jordan was styling Peter's hair. 'It looks a bit like my mate Gatesy,' she said, a clear reference to the *Pop Idol* star Gareth Gates, with whom she'd once had a fling after she and Dwight has parted company, while she was pregnant with Harvey. The viewers never knew what Peter said to that, because his reply was such that the producers hastily turned the sound off. But he didn't look very pleased, first apologising to Jordan, and then storming off. Immediately, Jordan declared she didn't fancy him, because he was 'too stroppy'.

'He's lost the plot,' said Kerry, who had witnessed the whole thing. 'He's jealous, he is. He is very immature. I can't believe he's thirty.'

The scrapping went on for a bit. Jordan confided in Alex Best that she thought Peter was only playing up to her for publicity. He, in turn, was very upset. 'I don't understand why you are being like that,' he said, only for Jordan to tell him, 'I need time to think.'

'Have it your way. It does not bother me at all,' said Peter. But it clearly did.

Alex was voted off next, while Jordan and Peter continued to bicker. The rest of the camp started to ask Jordan what was really going on in their relationship.

'I'm not doing anything wrong,' she said, before adding rather bluntly, 'People have got to realise that we are in here and there's no one else about.'

Peter, unsurprisingly, was none too pleased about this, saying, 'Don't give that shit, as if I'm a piece of chopped liver – we care about each other.'

'I think Pete really likes you,' Kerry interjected.

'It's just fun turning into something he's really fallen for,' said Jordan dismissively.

'Why don't you just say the truth and stop trying to make me look stupid?' demanded Peter in turn.

'It's like I've been watching a couple who've been married for five years,' Kerry beamed.

Although Jordan was as popular as she ever had been with the viewing public, it was beginning to seem as if she wouldn't win, after all. Following the departure of John Lydon, it looked as if Lord Brocket was in with a chance, but, after he launched a very outspoken attack against Jennie Bond, he, too, was deemed to have little chance. Increasingly, despite constant tears and her own threats to quit throughout the show, it seemed as if it would be Kerry who marched off with the crown, as indeed proved to be the case.

However, Jordan had managed to make it through to the top five. 'Every day someone you don't think is going to leave the camp goes,' she told presenters Ant and Dec. 'I keep saying it doesn't matter. Alex was the cook, the cleaner, getting logs. It just goes to show it doesn't matter how "in" to the group you look like you're being, it doesn't mean to say you're staying in. I'm quite lazy and I admit it, but that's just me. I didn't think I would be in the top five. People hate me at home, don't they? So, I'm lucky I'm still here.'

Ant and Dec assured her that she absolutely was not hated at home – and, indeed, she was still there.

At this point, Jordan was forced to undergo her fourth (and last) Bushtucker Trial. Navigating her way across water on logs, she was to collect a number of snakes and eels from Perspex boxes. Given that she had cited, among other phobias, snakes, eels and water, this was more of a trial than usual, but she managed to collect three meals for the campers, as well as a treat.

Sadly, there was yet another spat with Peter. Again, perhaps a forerunner of what was to come.

'Let me tell you something, right, that was enough for me,' said Peter. 'Now there's nothing. I'm not interested… It took that for me to realise you've been playing a game.'

Jordan promptly accused Peter of suggesting they go to the pool in a bid to 'win the game'.

'Wait,' he replied. 'No, I didn't say anything about winning the game.'

'So, I thought all along it's a game,' said Jordan.

'Listen to me,' said Peter, clearly upset now. 'I did not say it's a game… You're full of shit! Listen to me, right. Everything I said to you was genuine and can I tell you something? Well, I'm not interested, mate. I don't care any more. Do you know why? Because one thing I don't need in my life is games. I'm a bit too old for that.'

Jordan walked off, saying, 'I'm not arguing. Get me out of here, someone.'

'Why can't you just let a discussion finish?' asked Peter. 'I've got to clear it up because I really want to go.'

It was setting a pattern for their rows in years to come.

And with that, Jordan was voted off (ironically, some people believed this was because the public perceived her to be toying with Peter's affections). Wearing a white tutu, she left the camp, telling Ant and Dec that she was relieved to go as tensions had been building up between everyone still in the game. What the outside world was really curious to know about, though, was the exact nature of her relationship with Peter. On this, Jordan was a bit coy.

'I was warned about Peter before I got in there, but he's a nice guy,' she said. 'There's nothing going on with him. He's gorgeous, good-looking, the type I'd go for. If he does want to go for dinner, we can, but I'm not saying anything will come of it. If he is in the country, then he can stay at mine.'

Peter himself didn't appear to know what to make of it. 'I love the person that I met here when she didn't turn into that other person,' he told the remaining celebrities in the camp. 'She was her sweet self – I love that. I was actually really, really feeling something, you know. I guess this is life, man. I think last night was enough for me after we spoke and I realised that maybe this was all just bullshit. It's because I genuinely liked her, but she didn't believe me and that was what was frustrating. So, today I pulled her aside and I spoke to her, and she didn't like it but I told her what I thought – I told her I'm not into games, I like things straight.

'Everything I said to her I meant but she won't believe that. She doesn't want to believe it. That's the bit that hurts me that I meant it.'

However, everything would be sorted out soon enough.

There was, of course, the minor matter of one Scott Sullivan. He had flown out to Australia to be with his girlfriend, but after all that on-screen cavorting with Peter, and whatever Jordan might be saying then, clearly something had been going on. Could the relationship be rescued?

'I'm devastated by what Katie's been up to with Peter,' admitted Scott in the *Sunday Mirror*, shortly before she left the programme. 'It's eating away at me all the time – the thought of whether it's all an act for the cameras or if there's something really going on. What's worse is that I'm sure Katie must realise what she's doing is going to upset me, but she doesn't seem to care. I'm still clinging to the hope that this is all a stunt and part of her game plan to win.'

It was certainly a bit of a mess, and one that needed to be resolved. By now, the couple had been together for eighteen months and the relationship had been serious, in its way.

'I don't know what's going to happen between us,' Scott continued. 'I hope we can work it out, but, no matter how far she goes, I'll forgive her. Katie's just too special to me to let go of without a fight. We've always had a rocky relationship, but as far as I was concerned, it was serious. I hate the whole celebrity scene that surrounds us – it can cause problems. It's like going out with two different people: Katie, who is really special to me, and her alter-ego Jordan, who I can't stand. But sometimes Jordan can get in the way of things – which is what I think might be happening now.'

Strangely enough, Peter had also just confessed that he, too, had seen the Jordan side of Katie's character and was also none too keen, but it was Scott who was agonising now.

'I desperately hope we can get the relationship back on track,' he said. 'But at the moment I've moved back in with my parents so we can have some space when she gets out.

'It's really frustrating not being able to speak to her face to face and find out what is going on. I've decided not to go to the show when she comes out as I want to talk to her in private about what's been going on. I don't want the whole thing turned into a media side show.'

Ant and Dec, no less, had added their own voices to what was going on: it was, they said, no more than a fling that would fall apart outside the jungle. But they were wrong. For a start, Jordan was heard outside the camp calling out that she missed Peter.

'I miss her too,' was his response. '[But] I'm gonna stay single for a while... I get too involved and I don't like it. She's obviously got lots of issues she's got to sort out. I'm one of these people, I might not trust easily but, once I let someone in, it's quite rapid. Once feelings are involved, I prefer to keep it that way. So, yes, I've got a lot of stuff to sort out in my head.'

Lord Brocket was the next to leave – although he had never really been a serious contender to win the show, he had provided great entertainment and been a really good sport.

And then Peter left. He continued to be reticent about the relationship, saying of Jordan, 'We really need to talk, me and her. We have got a lot to discuss. She is a lovely girl. I will always say nice things about her. She just happens to be attractive as well.'

Jordan was doing some thinking, too, and it was pretty clear the way her mind was working. Scott, it seemed, was now well and truly out of the picture.

'I had a boyfriend. Over. Gone. Don't want to know,' she said. 'I just said to him, "I don't want to speak any more." He said, "Is it over?" And I said, "Basically, yes." I think Peter is the absolute type I go for. He is the look I go for and the personality.'

She wouldn't have long to wait now.

Kerry was crowned Queen of the Jungle and, at the time, was at the height of her popularity – her wholesome good nature had endeared her to viewers and they clearly wanted to show her that back.

Meanwhile, Jordan had a revelation that stunned the

viewers: she and Peter had got much closer than they initially let on. 'Yes, Peter and I did get very intimate,' she admitted. 'The sexual tension between us was mind-blowing. I fought against it every single minute we were in there, but it was impossible to resist. I wanted him so much, it physically hurt. He's devastatingly sexy and I had to give in to my urges.'

And the cameras missed it – just.

'It happened when Peter crept into my bed one night,' she continued. 'I could feel him by my side and the temptation was unbelievable. Despite my jokes about Peter's "acorn", I knew instantly that we were both hungry for sex. The rules of the show are that you have to keep your microphones on all the time and, of course, there were cameras everywhere but nothing was going to stop me. The temptation just grew inside me.

'It was me who pulled his arm around me, but it was him who tightened it and tucked it under my boobs so he was even closer. It just felt right. I knew what he wanted, and, God, I was so much in the mood myself! His hands began to wander and temptation grew. I was desperate for him and let things go further than I ever thought I would.'

However, the two held off at the last moment. They heard a camera whirring nearby and realised that, if they carried on, they would actually be caught. That would not do.

'I know sour old boots like Posh Spice think I'm a

slapper, but I'm not,' said Jordan. 'I love sex, though, and don't see why I should be ashamed to admit that. The sheer physical pull between Peter and I made me forget everything else. I wanted, needed and had to have him. I am a mum, though, and wouldn't want to do anything that would make Harvey ashamed of me when he grows up. Hearing that camera move in the bush brought me to my senses.'

She was unforthcoming, though, on the subject of what *exactly* did go on.

'To a lot of people, it would be like having sex,' she said. 'I didn't want Peter to leave me that night, but it was starting to get light. It was the most sexually charged night of my life and I can't wait to be reunited with Peter so we can finally, totally, satisfy our passions.'

Finally, she was putting it on the line.

So was Peter. Now that the two of them had left the jungle, and realising the other was not playing a game, they could hardly wait to take their relationship further – this time with no cameras in sight. Indeed, they were sounding like nothing so much as overexcited teenagers, with Peter now confirming what Katie had told the world – that they'd taken things much further in the jungle than anyone realised at the time.

'The two of us got up close and personal in the camp,' Peter admitted. 'But that was just a taste of what's to come. I've had the starter, now I want the main course. I've fallen

74

Jordan's first ever photoshoot, the beginning of an astronomical rise to stardom.

Both Katie and Peter tasted success from an early age.

Australian-born Peter found success through his music, hitting the top of the UK charts with 'Mysterious Girl' and 'Flava'.

Neither Katie nor Peter could have predicted how much this reality TV show was going to change their lives.

Above: The entire cast of *I'm A Celebrity… Get Me Out of Here!* 2004.

Below: Katie and Peter flying into the jungle.

Will they or won't they? The nation watched with bated breath as Katie and Peter flirted their way through the jungle.

Katie and Peter officially became an item after the end of *I'm a Celebrity… Get Me Out of Here!*

Above: Katie found herself at the centre of media attention after her stint in the jungle, and sales of her autobiography, *Being Jordan*, skyrocketed.

Right: Peter Andre also tried to capitalise on the new-found attention by releasing a new single 'Insania', which Jordan was happy to promote in her own way!

Britain's hottest power couple: Jordan and Peter Andre set to take the world by storm.

for Katie like mad. She's a beautiful, amazingly sexy girl. I've got Jungle Fever and bedding her is the only cure.'

Of course, the romance was to go much further than that, with the two marrying in a fairytale ceremony just a year or so later. But, at the time, in that first flush of passion, it was the physical element on both their minds.

'I slipped into her bed at night several times,' Peter continued. 'I think there were quite a few times the cameras didn't pick up on. We didn't have full sex, but things got intimate, and very hot and heavy.'

It seemed, however, that the couple hadn't been aware of quite how much the cameras had picked up on.

'How clear were the night-time cameras?' Peter demanded, when told that the two of them were seen to be getting increasingly affectionate. 'And it's black in camp, it's pitch-black. We saw little red lights, which we thought might be infrared, but we didn't expect that. Yes, there was a night; I needed to tell Katie how I felt. The sexual tension was crackling and becoming unbearable, so I went and said it. If there's something I feel I should do, I do it. I was naughty, I got a bit overexcited. We got intimate, but didn't have sex.

'I don't know how the cameras didn't pick up on the other nights. One night just led into another, but we didn't go all the way. I'm a thirty-year-old single guy, I don't know what to say. We got tantalisingly close, but that's it.'

Yet again, there was a warning note in the middle of all

this. Peter was now quite able to see the two sides of Jordan's character, and it wasn't the one that made the headlines that he was falling for. Sweet Katie, not outrageous Jordan, was the woman he wanted to be with, but somehow he didn't seem to be able to take it on board that the two formed part of the whole.

'Katie's an awesome girl, I just hope she realises she doesn't have to be Jordan,' he went on. 'She can be herself and people will hopefully see that side of her. I saw it, so did everyone else in camp. I don't want anything to do with all that wild-child stuff.'

Indeed, it was to go under wraps for quite some time – before the acrimonious split and the return of Katie's wilder side.

CHAPTER FIVE

KATIE – AND JORDAN

One reason, perhaps, why Peter didn't seem to be able to see that Jordan really did have two sides to her personality was that, before the jungle, he'd been unaware of her notoriety. Since his career as a pop singer had gone into decline back in 1998, when he was dropped by his record label, he hadn't spent much time in the UK, which meant that his first experience of Jordan was as Katie, as it were. He hadn't known the history of her very public, and usually doomed, liaisons, the falling out of nightclubs barely dressed, and all the other antics for which she had become known. He saw the real Jordan, or, rather, Katie, for sure, but he didn't fully comprehend the other side to her character – and it was there, for all that she had built Jordan up to play a part.

In some ways, Pete was beginning to realise this. 'When

I landed in England, it was like, "This is the girl on the front cover of the papers every day – you're going into the jungle with her,"' he recalled. 'When we first met, she came up to me and was really brash and said, "All right, mate?" I just thought, "Nah, love, you're not for me." I was quite relieved as I didn't want to fancy anyone in there. She put on a front, always teasing me and trying to act all hard, like kids at school. But they always say, when girls are horrible to you, it means they fancy you: I didn't expect us to click.'

It has often happened, though, that people, especially celebrities, build up a façade they have throughout most of their lives and, in the 24-hour glare of the camera, that was what happened in this particular story. Katie couldn't be Jordan 24/7, and so she reverted to who she really was. It was to be the making of her, significantly boosting her popularity with the public at large – while, at the same time, Pete began to fall in love.

'I was surprised at seeing her other side, the sweeter side,' he revealed. 'I was surprised to see a much nicer person than I'd heard about. Whatever I said in there, I genuinely meant. She didn't believe a lot of it, but I *did* mean it. And I didn't say it for any other reason apart from the fact I liked the nice side of Katie.'

There was another ominous moment, as well: the duo had only seen one another once since the show ended: at the party during which Kerry was crowned Queen of the

Jungle. Jordan was sporting a new blonde hairdo, and plenty of make-up – in other words, her normal look. But Peter didn't like it. 'I wanted to scrape all the make-up off,' he said. 'It looks horrible. I like girls to look natural.' It was, however, the way Katie liked to appear.

Funnily enough, Ant and Dec appeared to understand this. They were well acquainted with the Jordan of the London nightclub scene, and they could tell that the two different sides to her persona might come to grief in the end. While they were wrong in that they thought the relationship would turn out to be just a holiday fling, they were spot-on in realising that Peter had not seen the whole picture.

'I think she liked him chasing her and, instead of running, she stopped for a couple of days and let herself be caught,' said Ant.

'It's like a holiday romance – it's all because of the surroundings and then you go back home and think, What the hell have I done? and it's never the same,' added Dec. 'The girl he got to know there was Katie, not Jordan. Jordan isn't Katie when she goes back to London and hits Chinawhite.'

He was absolutely right, although it would be a long time before anyone realised the full truth of this – and, in fairness, the relationship did last quite a while longer than the average holiday romance.

Despite the fact that both were now making a song and

dance about how they wanted to be an item, there was some way to go before everything finally worked out. Still having had hardly any contact since leaving the jungle, the pair were separated when Jordan flew back to London, her mother Amy and baby Harvey in tow. Peter followed on shortly afterwards. Both were now inundated with offers of work, while Jordan herself, now well on the way to becoming Katie Price in the public eye, had discovered quite how her image had changed.

She was mobbed by fans at Heathrow, but they were quite different fans to the paparazzi and men keen to get it on with her that she was used to: this was middle England, out in force to meet their new heroine, and there were plenty of women in the crowd. Indeed, from then on, in a total change from the early days, the majority of the supporters were women, not men. But now the whole country loved her. Jordan had proven herself to be brave and gutsy in the jungle and now she was turning into a national icon as well.

'I'm amazed that all these people have taken the time to come and welcome me,' she said, clearly as taken aback as anyone else about what was going on.

However, Jordan and Peter were now back – or at least, in the same country – with all the opportunities provided by that. Peter had re-released his former nineties hit 'Mysterious Girl' and was due to perform on the BBC's *Top of the Pops* the following week (rumour was rife that Jordan would be his back-up singer). Both certainly had a fair bit to think about: not only their burgeoning relationship, but also just how they would deal with all the work now piling up on their plates.

There was still a touch of 'Will they?/Won't they?' about it all, although the eventual outcome was looking increasingly clear. Matters went a step further when Peter appeared on *CD:UK* with Cat Deeley and a massive bouquet of roses arrived. The card read: 'To Peter, you know you are my everything. Love Katie Price (NOT Jordan).' As the crowd went wild, Peter blushed and murmured, 'Unbelievable,' while Cat crowed, 'I feel like Cilla!' This was a real relationship now, no doubting that.

The only fly in the ointment was Scott Sullivan. Naturally, he had not taken his very public split with his girlfriend at all well. His mother Sally spoke out to criticise Jordan for leaving her son a wreck. 'Katie has made a fortune out of all this and Scott hasn't seen a penny,' she revealed to the *Sunday Mirror*. 'The truth is we've helped Katie and her mum out over the past eighteen months, now we are out of pocket. I know everyone says, "Scott the millionaire's son", but we are not as wealthy as people think.

'It has been a horrible time for all of us. I and the family have been through hell – I have had to stand by and feel as if I could do nothing when I knew my son was thousands of miles away, all alone. Katie knows how to deal with it all, but we have all been struggling. Scott is only a kid and has had to deal with everything on his own.'

But Jordan was falling in love and impervious to the rants. And, sad as it was for Scott, these things do happen: the couple were not even engaged, let alone married, and Katie was, to a certain extent, free to fall for whoever she pleased.

'My mind's made up,' she said in a television interview. 'He's [Scott] a lovely guy, but I'm besotted with Pete, unfortunately. I'll admit I've never felt like this about anyone – I am so into him. He's met Harvey in Australia, but I haven't had that much detail yet. Until we meet up and, you know... I can't wait. Maybe love is in the air – who knows?'

Who knew, indeed? Jordan was now taking it all so seriously that she was considering dumping the old public persona and bringing to light the other side of her instead. Until then, she had been Jordan, but now Katie Price was making her way to the stage – all because of Peter.

'Jordan is a slag, slut and bitch,' said Katie rather dramatically in the *Mirror*. 'Kate likes to stay at home, curl up in front of the fire and play with her son. The problem I've had is the Jordan side has started to take over my life. It's an act, but it's out of control. I realised that, if I'm going to make a relationship last, it's going to be as Kate, not Jordan. He has told me he's fallen for Kate, the real me. Not Jordan, the glamour girl I invented. She is gone... dead.

I want more children, a proper family with the man I love
– that's Peter.'

Although they had met up, the couple still had not
managed to spend any real quality time together since
leaving the jungle, but, from the way they were talking
about one another, it was obvious that both of them were
very serious indeed. Now it was Peter's turn to talk about
where their relationship was going next.

'I'll be over the moon if Jordan wants to get married and
have my babies,' he revealed. 'I'd marry her, but I'll have to
get to know her first because I don't know if she really
means it. She hardly knows me, though she got to know
me quite well in the jungle. I was taken aback by her yes-
no behaviour in the jungle, but I stuck to my guns. She
seems pretty awesome to me and I saw a side to her which
is amazing. We really need to talk. It's as simple as that.'

Of course, Jordan already had a son, Harvey, but that
didn't matter in the least to Peter. He came from Cypriot
stock, a background that prized family over everything,
and he was delighted to take the little boy into the equation
as well.

'When you really love someone, you accept them as a
package,' he said. 'I'm not worried about looking after
Harvey. He's great. I saw him in Australia and spent a bit of
time with him. He is a beautiful little boy. Jordan and I are
going to spend some quality time very soon. We discussed
that at a meeting we went to on Thursday night. It wasn't

a date, there were six people there. We are going to see each other soon because we know we can't leave it weeks or months if it is going to blossom.'

Things looked to be blossoming pretty fully as they were. The only reason why the couple were not actually able to spend more time together was the heavy schedule of promotional activities both had now embarked upon, with Peter's re-released 'Mysterious Girl' shooting up the charts. But there was much talk of the two of them taking a holiday together, in order to get to know one another more.

But progress was being made. Jordan introduced Peter to her parents, Amy and Paul, a sure sign that the relationship was serious, and, despite reports that Peter's parents Savvas and Thea were rather anxious about his linking up with a glamour model, he wished to do the same in return. Peter's record company was said to be worried for much the same reason, but this was mainly because they had yet to understand the massive shift in public opinion as far as Jordan was concerned. The days of falling out of nightclubs, as she herself had said, were over. From now on, it would be all change.

And now that they were managing to find time to be together, events moved fast. The couple gave a joint magazine interview in which Peter appeared to be asking Katie to move in with him, adding, 'It's serious, deep adult stuff. Waiting makes you want it more.' Not that they had to wait for anything now – the relationship was moving full steam ahead.

There was a small blip in the proceedings when, forgetting Jordan's past digs at Victoria Beckham, Peter somewhat unwisely called the former Spice Girl 'cute' in a radio interview, but he hastily made amends, saying, 'If me and Jordan end up in a relationship, it's going to end up being between me and Beckham, isn't it? I'm gonna stick up for Jordan and he's gonna stick up for Posh.'

As expected, and fittingly, 'Mysterious Girl' hit the No. 1 slot in February 2004, yet another cause for celebration at the end of what had been a spectacular month for them both. Just a few weeks previously, Peter had been a forgotten pop star and Jordan a slightly downmarket glamour model – now the two of them were not only reaping huge professional success, but they were also fast on their way to becoming one of the most popular couples in Britain. Indeed, they threatened to rival the great Posh and Becks themselves.

Paul Price, Katie's stepfather, was delighted with the way things were going. They were now all but living together: Peter was spending half his time at Jordan's Sussex home, bonding with Harvey, and even going riding after Jordan had bought two horses for the duo.

'She has never really wanted to get married before, but Peter seems a great bloke and I think it's the real thing this time – particularly now they have moved in together,' Paul said in *Closer* magazine.

'It's really serious. Kate is closer to Peter than she was with any of her previous boyfriends. Peter also gets on brilliantly with Harvey; he dotes on him. Kate and Peter are very lovey-dovey together. All the right ingredients are there. There is no reason why, with such strong foundations, they shouldn't stay together for good. It's a proper, serious relationship and I hope it will end in marriage.'

And, of course, his wish was to be fulfilled. Jordan and Peter had by now turned into Katie and Pete: for the next few years they would be inseparable. But just who were they, and where did they come from, this couple who were by now attracting such fascination? And how did they get to where they are today?

CHAPTER SIX

KATIE AND PETE STEP OUT

In the wake of *I'm A Celebrity...*, interest in Katie and Pete reached fever pitch. It wasn't just that the public perception of the two of them had changed profoundly in the course of a few weeks, it was also the fact that the whole nation had witnessed them falling in love that was so intriguing to all. Reality television has produced a few romances, but rarely any as high profile – and, indeed, unlikely – as this one. Where would it all end?

Early whispers that this could have been just a publicity stunt soon died down as it became apparent that the two really were besotted with one another; they were all but living together and surrounded by that inexplicable glow that happens when people are really in love. And they were. In early March, the two were spotted visiting the London restaurant Hakkasan to celebrate Pete's 31st birthday; Katie was wearing a very ostentatious ring on her engagement finger. Could they be engaged after such a short time?

Well, no, but they were blissfully happy together, that much was clear. And the change of image continued apace. Katie was now being represented by Claire Powell, also Pete's agent, who was guiding her into a much more salubrious sphere.

'Before *I'm A Celebrity...*, she couldn't believe anyone would be interested in Katie Price, it was all about Jordan,' said Claire, who was to play a profound role in turning Katie's image around. 'Jordan will still exist, but the only place she'll be doing topless modelling is in her own calendar. Otherwise, that period of her life is over.'

Nonetheless, the old sauciness was still very much in evidence. Katie turned up to a photoshoot wearing a tracksuit that bore the legend 'Golden Balls'. This, as everyone knew, was Victoria Beckham's nickname for David. Clearly, she wasn't ready to let old rivalries die down just yet.

The photoshoot for the jacket of Katie's first autobiography, *Being Jordan*, was being taken by Terry O'Neill, a society photographer far more closely associated with an up-market image that Katie had not really embraced until now. But it was all part of the new image. 'I have to admit I am more used to movie stars, but these days, in Britain, Jordan is a better-known name

KATIE AND PETE STEP OUT

than Ava Gardner,' said Terry. 'Her team wanted a classic look so we had her looking more natural, her hair loose and wavy. She's a girl who sees she's got so many years left and is working hard at it. She's right to make the move into more mainstream work because modelling has a limited shelf-life.'

In the meantime, the relationship was coming on in leaps and bounds. It was not just Katie and Pete who were getting on, either. Already Pete was forming a strong bond with Harvey, so much so that the little boy was soon coming to consider him to be his own father. A trip to the shops was proof of that.

'Peter was acting like the model dad,' said an onlooker. 'While Jordan nipped into clothes shops, he pushed Harvey round the block to keep the baby amused or get him off to sleep. And when she came back, it wasn't as if he was in a hurry to hand the buggy back to her. He seemed so happy just to play dad.'

Sadly, this would only add to the poignancy of the parting five years later. Pete is, to an extent, the only father Harvey has known, but, since the link is not a biological one, the legal situation is cloudier.

Even though her image was changing so dramatically, remnants of the old Jordan were still there. Katie had been Jordan for quite a while, after all, and couldn't expect the past to be brushed away that quickly. Despite her undisputed happiness with Pete, an old boyfriend still crept out of the woodwork to do a kiss and tell. Dreadlocked show jumper Oliver Skeete told of a night of passion that had taken place when Katie was just nineteen. 'She was wearing high heels, a tiny miniskirt and no knickers,' he said. 'How the hell could I refuse?'

Katie rose above it all and didn't dignify his story with a comment. In fact, she even showed some willingness to heal the rift with Victoria Beckham despite the much-circulated story that Victoria had burst into a rendition of 'Who Let the Dogs Out?' when, some years previously, the two of them were present in the Manchester United hospitality rooms. This was around the time when David was alleged to have had an affair with Rebecca Loos, and Katie showed some sympathy.

'A lot has happened between us,' she said. 'But I'm an adult now, I can forgive her, and I'd like to make up with her; she probably needs a shoulder to cry on.'

Katie was not, however, as conciliatory to Jodie Marsh. Jodie was also a glamour model who had been trying to follow in Katie's (or rather, Jordan's) footsteps, with hardly the same degree of success. It emerged that she had been seeing none other than Scott Sullivan. 'I wish her so much luck,' said Katie icily. 'They suit each other so well.'

Meanwhile, her own relationship continued to go well, although Pete was keen to scotch rumours they were engaged. 'We aren't getting married and it's rubbish that I am going to propose to her,' he said wearily. 'There is nothing like that going on. We haven't talked about marriage yet. There is a lot I won't talk about and a lot I keep personal; there are things I don't need to say and we'll see what happens. But there is no talk of engagement or marriage – I don't know where that came from.' Possibly the showy, engagement-style ring Katie had been sporting, but no matter.

There was still the odd suggestion that they were together for the publicity angle and nothing else and that annoyed Pete, too. 'People can think what they want, but time will tell and people will see that, when two people care for each other, they want to go under the same management, they want to have schedules so that they can spend more time together,' he said. 'I'm not in a hurry to prove anything to anybody. It's early days; it's only been three months and it is plain to see we are fond of each other. There's no rush, we are just getting to know each other. We've been seeing each other and we're on the phone every day. There hasn't been a day we haven't spoken since the jungle.'

Indeed, the bond between them was palpably growing. And perhaps it wasn't such a surprising match after all: both were well aware of the tough side of the world in which they lived, both had made their names because of their striking appearances, as well as – in Pete's case – his singing talent, and both were deeply aware of the importance of family. Indeed, Harvey could well have been one of the reasons why such a strong bond existed between them, for Pete was impressed by the way Katie had coped with having a disabled child and all the love and affection she lavished on him. Katie, meanwhile, was similarly taken by the way Pete behaved around Harvey. Whatever the truth, the fact is that the three of them increasingly resembled a tight-knit family bond.

Meanwhile, Pete, as much as Katie, was incredibly aware of the new lease of life the jungle had given him – and was grateful for it, too. But he wasn't taking anything for granted. He had tasted both the highs and the lows of the business once more and was well aware that it could all disappear tomorrow – as, indeed, it once had. This time around, he simply intended to take advantage of the opportunities offered to him and to enjoy the ride. And, certainly, it was one in the eye for everyone who'd said he was finished, something he couldn't help but relish.

'What a surprise how things have changed,' he said. 'Because I've been there and done it before, I know not to get caught up the hype. I got caught up in it 200 per cent the last time. It was the first round of success. It all hit me, the money and power. All of a sudden I could call the shots and make things happen the way I wanted them to happen. I didn't see it ending. I thought, I'm making good money and I'm always going to have it. Then it was taken away.'

He had clearly learned a lot from that first shot at

stardom, and sounded a considerably older and wiser man. 'I always felt I was good to people, but I believed in my own hype,' he admitted. 'It all worked but, when I stepped away from it, I realised fame is an illusion. It's a fickle business and I now know it. I made a comeback nobody thought was possible and made it to No. 1. Everything else is an added bonus.'

It was, indeed, a huge turnaround from the recent past. Before the jungle, although not actually broke, Pete had certainly been nowhere near as wealthy as he'd been in his heyday. Now work and money was flooding in. Not only had his musical career taken off again but offers for endorsements and promotional appearances were flooding in. From being a bit of a joke, Pete had become hot property and he was certainly having the last laugh now.

And then there were those abs... Rather endearingly, Pete also seemed a little embarrassed about the continuing emphasis on his physique. 'I don't want it to sound like I loved myself, but I had an image that was threatening – this image of always working out at the gym and always bronzed, and always watching what I eat,' he said. 'That's threatening or intimidating to any average person who just wants to enjoy life. When you train your arse off, people think it's implants; when you prove to them it's not implants, they say it's vanity. When you decide you're not going to work out any more, they say you've let yourself go.'

Those were the words of a man who had been there, done that and seen it all before. But before, Pete had never been able to enjoy the kind of relationship he was now beginning to build with Katie, either in his previous period of success or at any other time. In the past, he'd been too young, but, having suffered the travails of recent years, he was now mature enough to know that good relationships come along only rarely, and that he now had the possibility of just that on his hands.

In short, he was far more relaxed than he had been before. 'I thought, You know what, I will never please everybody, and what ultimately makes me happy is going out with my friends, going out for coffee or to a bar for a drink and to relax,' he said. 'That, to me, is the image I portray now. In the jungle, people saw that I wasn't a threat. I didn't come across in a vain manner and people felt they could relate. I've come back.

'I could easily turn around and say, "Ha, ha, up yours!" to everybody who didn't believe in me, but I don't. I say, so what? I've come back and I'm really appreciative of those who believe. What do I care of people who don't believe? I know that it is a fickle business and I'm appreciative of the support I get. However long it lasts, one thing's for sure, I'm enjoying it.'

And they both were. More in demand than ever, Pete was heading up the charts again with his next single, 'Insania', with speculation mounting that the two might do a duet.

'This time I feel a lot better,' he said. 'I am more relaxed and easy-going, and I now understand and appreciate the business. I've learned not to get caught up in my own hype. I've been wise this time and invested money, so if it does all end tomorrow I'll be fine. I wanted to come back one more time and see if I could get a No. 1 single and I did it. A lot of people dissed me, but people say the best revenge is to be successful. I don't feel I need to prove anything any more.'

Meanwhile, Katie was doing everything she could to support him, too. When Pete was out signing records, she accompanied him all the way. And still the rumours of a duet continued. 'I would love to write for other people,' he said. 'Most of all, I love to sing R&B and soul, but, when I write, I know I'm best at writing pop. I would write for soul artists and I would love to write for Kate, if she wanted me to.'

Katie herself was also doing very well professionally. She had done a stint on ITV's *Hell's Kitchen* in 2004 and was in demand wherever she went, but it was obvious that she was also thoroughly enjoying supporting Pete. The two of them shot a video to support his single, 'Love You The Right Way', to be released in the autumn of 2004, which had the two of them writhing on a bed and a beach.

'I didn't want any other woman to get that close to my man,' purred Katie.

'I didn't want to be that intimate with anyone but Kate,' breathed Pete. 'It really was a beautiful thing, making the video with the woman that I love. After having Katie in the film, anyone else would be a step backwards. I would maybe consider having a nice couple in my next video – but working with other glamour models on my own is now a definite no-no.'

It was also another sign that the two worked well together, professionally as well as personally. The relationship had moved up yet another gear.

The next rethink was the size of her breasts: did the FF image really suit the new Katie? For the first time, a possible reduction was spoken about.

'Katie is deadly serious about becoming more respectable,' said a source. 'She hasn't been seen falling out of clubs for months, she's been posing for far fewer raunchy shots, and she wants everyone to see that she's settling down. She feels that the ridiculously oversized breasts are the last thing holding her back from changing her public image.'

A holiday in the Maldives followed. Again, it was very different from what had gone before. So, was this really love? It was certainly beginning to look like it, not least because Katie was starting to sound positively dreamy when it came to Pete. The holiday was totally different from anything she's done before and she had enjoyed every minute of it. 'We play Scrabble and gin rummy – and I love it,' she said, sounding as astonished as everyone else. 'Usually with guys, I've just wanted to go clubbing, always on the lookout for something better. But with Pete I don't have to go out. I'm happy to stay in and play cards. It's nice for the first time it's not all about sex. That's a big part of it, but I don't feel like I have to do it.'

Until now, Pete's parents, Thea and Savvas, had reportedly been a little cautious about their son's new flame. But, by August, reports were beginning to circulate that Katie and Pete had taken part in the Loyasmeni tradition, a Greek courtship ritual in which the couple seek permission from their parents to marry. This put the relationship on a whole new footing, with the clear implication that they would do just that, and it also marked a change in the way the Andreas saw Katie. If she was prepared to embrace their son's Greek heritage, then they were equally happy to have her in their family.

Katie and Pete were certainly happy to tease each other in public, as became clear when the now highly sought-after Pete was asked to sing at the Miss Scotland finals at the SECC in Glasgow in September that year. 'Katie has told me in no uncertain terms that I'd better keep my hands to myself – or else!' said a good-natured Pete. 'I've always had an eye for gorgeous Scots girls and to be mixing with a dozen of the best-looking babes in the country will be a dream. I have tried to explain that I'm a good boy these days, but she's been bending my ear that I'll be in deep, deep trouble if I'm not on my best behaviour. Katie has even threatened to take a day off from her own work to come to the finals and act as a chaperone.'

Of course, Katie herself was not exactly a slouch in the glamour stakes, something her boyfriend was only too happy to make clear. 'I would really like to have been a judge at the competition so I could cast my eye properly over the girls,' said Pete. 'I doubt if any of them will be quite as big up top as Katie, but not many women are. In fact, they'd probably have to stick a few haggis suppers down their swimsuit tops to get anywhere close to the size of my woman.' Quite.

However, he did have his own views on what made a glamour girl stand out. 'But, to me, there's a lot more to being a successful beauty queen than just eye-popping physical attributes,' he explained. 'Sure, you need to be stunning, as I'm sure all the Miss Scotland finalists will be. But it's a killer smile and a dazzling personality that really counts, and that's what I want to see – honest!' In the event Katie did accompany him to the show, although by all accounts she seemed a little bad-tempered.

In all the excitement, it had almost been forgotten that Pete was not actually resident at that point in the UK and technically he was still living in Cyprus. But, in yet another sign of the growing depth of the relationship, that, too, was about to change. However, in other ways the couple's huge profile did appear to be taking its toll. Katie lashed out at a cameraman, Steve Lawrence, and had to attend court in September. Outside the courtroom, though, it was Pete who lost his rag, lashing out at reporters, calling them 'dogs', and adding, 'You'll pay! People know who you are and where you live.'

'The incident was bizarre, he just went potty,' said one, Gary Lucken, who had witnessed the scene. 'Then he challenged us to take him on "two to one". He is surprisingly intimidating for a small bloke. We declined the offer of a punch-up.'

Lawrence, whose camera Katie was accused of smashing, was equally bemused. 'I don't know why he got so irate – he's used to being in the public eye and this was a public street,' he said.

Ultimately, the case against Katie was dropped due to lack of evidence.

There was an equally bad-tempered scene at the 2004 *GQ* Awards at London's Royal Opera House, which Katie and Peter attended to present Matt Lucas and David Walliams of *Little Britain* fame with an award for Best Comedians. Also present was Anne-Marie Mogg, a runner-up in Miss Great Britain, who was unwise enough to flirt with Peter.

Katie did not take it well. 'Peter was deep in conversation with me, asking where such an exotic-looking girl like me came from,' Anne-Marie recalled. 'Jordan said, "I heard you're showing some flesh tonight. Turn around." Then she said, "Don't you think you need a bit of lipo?" I complimented her on her figure and she told me, "It's much better than yours." When they were leaving, Peter turned to kiss my cheek to say goodbye and she told me, "Get off my man."'

But there was another downside to all this, too. Scott Sullivan, clearly still smarting from his very public humiliation earlier in the year, chose to do a kiss and tell on his ex, in which he compared Katie's performance in bed with Jodie Marsh. Not for the first time, Katie was forced to rise above it all.

But there was plenty to celebrate, as well. In October, it was announced that the couple were to star in the first of many reality-TV shows featuring the two of them; cameramen had been following them since they had left the jungle and the results were to be screened in November. They would be paid £1 million for their participation in *When Peter Met Jordan*, and ITV was, rightly, very excited about its coup.

'ITV1 are really excited because they think it will be massive,' said a source. 'The nation is fascinated by Jordan, whether they love or hate her. People will get to know the truth about their relationship. The show will be must-see TV – it could be as big as *The Osbournes*. Despite what people think, they are in a proper relationship – it's not a publicity stunt.'

Indeed not: in fact, by then, the couple were formally engaged. 'Our marriage will last forever – as long as he doesn't cheat on me,' said the bride-to-be.

They flew to Miami, followed, as ever, by the cameras for

an engagement celebration cruise. Katie was wearing a huge ring and they confirmed that the wedding would take place the following year.

In the meantime, the next series of *I'm A Celebrity...* had begun to air. Katie and Pete, the previous series' most high-profile contestants, were called on for their point of view. Katie duly obliged. 'When you first go into camp, you're convinced you can get it sussed,' she said of the cameras that would be watching their every move. 'Me and Peter believed we'd worked out which were filming and which were switched off – which is why we got caught out on the night vision. The show producers are very sneaky: they realised everyone was sussing out the cameras, so they put fake lights on some and switched off lights on the ones which were filming. It's impossible to hide. I think everyone goes into the jungle thinking they know what to expect – I did. But, once you've been in a few days, you're all light-headed and half-starving and detoxing from booze and coffee and sugar, you drift into this state where you forget everything except what you are feeling.'

Celebrities were queuing up to get into the series. Hardly surprising, given the financial success Katie and Pete had enjoyed. They were raking it in, from books and television appearances, so much so, in fact, that Katie was able to buy a new six-bedroom farmhouse in Maresfield for £750,000. She was also reported to have bought a Ferrari for Pete, for their first Christmas together.

Planning for the wedding had also begun in earnest, with Katie announcing that she wanted to get married in a pink castle, after she'd seen one in Disneyland, Paris. 'We did ask if it was possible to get married there, but they said no,' she explained.

In the midst of it all, there was still family to worry about. Harvey had been treated with growth hormone injections, but reacted badly, vomiting and losing weight. He was taken to Brighton's Royal Alexandra Hospital in February 2005, where a concerned Katie stayed to be with him. However, on a more positive note, although he had been born blind, he had developed limited close-up vision, and, after a couple of days, he was allowed to go home.

If truth be told, Pete's singing career was not going as well as expected. His third single since leaving the jungle, 'The Right Way', went nowhere fast, and ticket sales for a concert tour were not looking like a sell-out. Rather surprisingly, Katie seemed to decide to adopt the mantle of singer in the family, instead.

Katie had chosen to compete for the chance to represent Britain in the Eurovision Song Contest. Eurovision had become a byword for a rather cheesy prime-time entertainment much beloved by the British public, but, even so, there was still some disbelief when Katie announced she wanted to take part. There had, perhaps, been more unlikely entrants, but none immediately sprung to mind. That didn't matter, though, for Katie was really prepared to do her bit and was very determined, at this stage at least, that Eurovision was the right place for her to go.

She was singing a song called 'Not Just Anybody' and was bullish about her chances of winning. 'I think people should vote for me because I'm new to this,' she said brightly. 'The others have all been in talent shows before; they've all been in the music business. I should be given a chance to represent the country. The British public has really supported me in the last couple of years and I feel I want to give something back; the only way I can do that is by representing the country. I'm not going to try and use my body, that's the Jordan side. I'm going to be Katie Price.'

But she also admitted to having had her doubts. 'I wasn't sure I wanted to do Eurovision because of its cheesy reputation,' she confessed. The song was 'poppy, but different, too – it has a James Bond theme-song sound. Pete's heard the song and he likes it. All I can do is hope the nation backs me. And, if they don't, I'll just have to wear the flag instead of flying it.'

Even this unlikely news, however, was eclipsed by the bombshell that the duo dropped in mid-February: they were expecting a child, due in June 2005. Indeed, Katie was actually five months pregnant, but, given the problems she'd had previously, the couple did not want to go public with the news until they were certain everything was all right.

'We apologise for not confirming this information earlier but we have been awaiting the all-clear from a scan, which was only confirmed at lunchtime today, that the baby is well and healthy,' they said in a statement. 'This was of particular importance due to the health complications with baby Harvey. The new baby is due this summer. We are all looking forward to the new addition to the family and we are extremely happy.'

With wedding preparations also well under way, they had a great deal to be happy about and, given how well Pete had bonded with Harvey, there was already evidence about what a good father he would make.

'Katie and Peter are thrilled about the baby,' said a friend of the duo. 'It wasn't planned, but they're both really excited. They are so in love and they can't wait to get married. Katie is relieved that the doctors told her everything is OK with the pregnancy. She was naturally very worried, given all of Harvey's problems.'

Delighted as they were, Pete's traditional side came out. He did, after all, come from a conservative Mediterranean background and, bad boy that he once was or not, he had a sense of propriety, of the way things should be done.

'I really want to get married as soon as possible after the baby,' he said. 'Ideally for me, we would have got married before we had a child. It's the wrong way round, but, you know, these things happen.'

Katie was a little more laidback. 'It certainly was not

planned, but we weren't exactly careful either,' she said. 'But we know we will be together forever. We're not kids, we're not getting any younger, and we knew we wanted babies together at some point. I know loads of people will think we've rushed into everything, but I don't think there's a timescale for these things. Just why do you have to be together for years before getting married or having kids? It's just not like that these days. I say, if it feels right, you should go for it.'

So they did.

Preparations for Eurovision continued apace. Along with Katie, the other contestants were Gina G, Andy Scott-Lee, Javine and Tricolore, all singing in the BBC1 programme *Making Your Mind Up*. It was an interesting crew.

Gina G was an Australian, who was no stranger to Eurovision, having come seventh in the contest in 1996 with 'Ooh Ahh... Just A Little Bit'. The single got to No. 1 in the UK charts and she had two more hits, 'I Belong To You' and 'Fresh!'. After that, she'd faded from public view.

Andy Scott-Lee was the brother of former Steps singer Lisa Scott-Lee, and started out in boy band 3SL with his brothers Ant and Steve, who eventually parted company with their record label. Though ultimately voted off, he got to the last twelve in the second series of ITV's *Pop Idol* in 2003. He was dating another singer, Michelle Heaton, from Liberty X. 'Guardian Angel', his Eurovision entry, was written by Lee from another boy band, Blue.

Javine tried out for Girls Aloud, but didn't make the final five on the reality show *Popstars: The Rivals*. She went on to have a solo career and reached No. 4 in the charts with 'Real Things', but didn't really manage much of a career after that. She did, however, manage to incur Katie's ire, with Katie calling her a 'silly cow'.

Last, but not least, was Tricolore, a group of three tenors comprising Scott Ciscon, Jem Sharples and Stuart Pendred. They had sung alongside Sting and Beyoncé in the past, and performed for, among others, Eric Clapton, the Duchess of York and Lord Attenborough. Their album, *Beginnings*, came out in 2003.

This, then, was the competition. Katie had been practising singing and dancing lessons for months and was certainly a trouper. Her pregnancy was now showing, but she wasn't going to let that hold her back. Rather, as always, she was prepared to give it her all. But would that be good enough?

CHAPTER SEVEN

AND JUNIOR
MAKES FOUR

The nation was fixated on the screen. It was now just over a year since Katie Price had entered the jungle, and in doing so utterly changed her life. By this time, the nation was completely fascinated by her and Pete. Everything they did made the news, and they were doing a lot: apart from all the personal appearances, reality shows, interviews and single releases, Katie was taking on a brand-new challenge. Not only was she pregnant, but she was also fighting to enter the Eurovision Song Contest.

She had been making a huge effort to prepare for it all behind the scenes and, courtesy of her relationship with Pete, was becoming very au fait with the music industry. She was to mount quite a spectacle, that was for sure.

Katie herself, always able to stir up controversy, whatever she did, was scathing about the other

KATIE AND PETER – TOO MUCH IN LOVE

contestants on *Making Your Mind Up* – who, in turn, had been none too complimentary about her. 'The bitching has really begun in the camp – against me,' she declared to the *Sun*. 'Javine said I shouldn't enter because I'm pregnant and Gina G's been just as bitchy, going on about my boob job, as if having big boobs is a crime. She's obviously just ridiculously jealous. I can only imagine they're running scared to be so pathetic and are worried I've so much support.'

And she certainly had that – Katie's popularity was growing in leaps and bounds. She wasn't going to let anyone knock her down, either. There was also, of course, the issue of her pregnancy: it wasn't that usual for contestants to be five months pregnant, but, then again, why not?

But the sniping continued. 'It just makes me even more determined to win,' said Katie of the rivalry behind the scenes. 'The greatest thing in the world for me would be being able to wave to all the bitches after beating them. When I found I was pregnant, I took advice and was told there was no reason not to go ahead. I had terrible morning sickness at the beginning – I was throwing up all day, every day in December – but I'm over that now. I've never felt fitter or healthier.'

Katie was glowing, even if the bump was becoming increasingly noticeable. She was also hiding any anxieties well: after the trauma surrounding Harvey's birth, neither she nor Pete would ever be entirely relaxed about the health of their new child until it was actually born, and so to have something else to worry about, namely Eurovision, was a useful diversion. And at any rate, everything seemed to be fine.

It certainly didn't seem to be a reason for Katie to hide herself away. 'Being pregnant isn't a problem for me,' she continued. 'I think it's something to celebrate – the first-ever pregnant Eurovision entry. I can also sing, I'm sexy and I tell it like it is; that makes me ideal to represent Britain.'

Naturally, she would have been quite a controversial choice. If truth be told, the country was only just beginning to get used to the new-look Katie, as flamboyant as her alter-ego Jordan, but with rather less flesh on display. However, even those who had previously looked down on her were really beginning to warm to her; it seemed Pete had brought out a whole different side.

And Pete, of course, was the key to it all. At that stage, the couple were blissfully happy together and, in the way of couples in a relationship that is working well, their support for each other showed through in everything they did. If Pete felt any reservations about Katie entering what, until then, had been his territory, he certainly didn't show it. Rather, he supported his wife-to-be and encouraged her to get on that stage.

Although she had been Katie Price, as opposed to

Jordan, for the best part of a year now, Katie also felt Eurovision was a way of highlighting her new persona. She had the choice of going at it full-on in glamour model mode, or trying to be taken seriously as a dancer and it was the latter she went for.

'I'm doing this as Katie Price – me, myself, I – not Jordan,' she said. 'It's the first time I've done anything as just Katie. My routine will be in-your-face, but in a good way. I'm proving I can sing and deserve to be given a chance. It's live, so there's nowhere to hide. I'm really nervous, which is the hardest to deal with. I can't help having this picture in my mind of millions of people staring at the TV while I'm up there.'

On the night itself, introduced by Terry Wogan as about to 'burst into song', the visibly pregnant Katie strutted her stuff in a skin-tight pink cat-suit, amid a troupe of dark-clad male dancers, but she narrowly missed top place, in a performance that was spirited, if occasionally a touch off-key. That honour went to Javine, singing 'Touch My Fire', who had a slight wardrobe malfunction, as her dress slipped to reveal more than it should during an energetic rendition of her song. Katie, unusually for her, came in second place.

It was not like Katie not to get her way: when she set her mind on getting something, she tended to achieve it, and so this was a blow. And Katie, who had been the bookies' favourite to win, was not best pleased and suspected the fact that she would be eight months pregnant in May, when the contest was staged, might have had something to do with the decision.

'I lost because I'm pregnant,' she said firmly. 'I gave it my best shot, I proved that I was committed and I had huge support. It's the only reason I can think of that certain people didn't want me because I wouldn't look slinky and sexy by the time of Eurovision. It's sick to think that, but I'm over it.'

It was, if truth be told, one of those rare moments in which she misjudged the public. When she took to the stage, she had been visibly shocked by some booing from the audience and looked stunned when she realised she wasn't going to win, after all. Katie was successfully turning her image around, but her voice was not her best asset and it had always been an unusual career decision for her to make. On the upside, though, it showed, yet again, that the woman had guts. She was prepared to expose herself to ridicule – and at least she had a go.

Kate was, however, very disappointed, and characteristically unable to hide it. 'I was gutted,' she said. 'I was the only one who entered the competition without a music career behind me and I genuinely wanted to win. It wasn't my greatest performance – I was nervous and wobbly at the beginning, but I can't believe that stopped people from voting for me.'

The sniping behind the scenes had been intense –

although Katie herself was no slowcoach when it came to having her say – and that didn't help matters either. Javine, meanwhile, was delighted. 'It takes talent to capture the public's attention, not just a lot of hype,' she announced rather gleefully. 'Jordan's campaign was based around her saying she'd win, so it must have been embarrassing for her to come second. At the end of the day, it's about talent and I'm a better singer. She still managed to come second, but I'm not going to comment on her actual singing.'

She did, however, relent a little after that, adding, 'Jordan's all right for someone who has never performed in front of millions. She was brave to put herself in that position.'

In fact, Katie appeared rather disappointed at the end of the show. She didn't attend the after-show party amid reports that she was too upset to do so; she herself merely let it be known that she was too tired to put in an appearance.

But she had had setbacks in the past, and had learned to deal with them, just as she would deal with this one now. Initially, Katie resolved to take it on the chin. 'Eurovision was just a test-run for my future career,' she said a few months later. 'I got a lot of stick for it, but I enjoyed the whole experience and that's what it was about for me. But it's nowhere near the type of music I am doing now. In fact, I now have a studio at home so I am up every day recording songs that I'm going to be releasing soon.'

In time, however, she would change her mind. Not only did Katie not like to fail, she also didn't like to feel that she'd made an idiot of herself – and, despite the size of her breasts, her extravagant outfits and a love of pink that would put Barbie to shame, she had rarely done so. Eurovision, though, was different. She had not appeared at her best and she had given the numerous people who liked to take a pop at her more ammunition than usual. 'I don't regret anything, apart from Eurovision,' she declared some years later. 'That is it; that's the worst thing I've ever done in my life.'

Meanwhile, she and Pete appeared to be more in love than ever, with her husband-to-be emphasising that he found her sexier by the day. Katie's pregnancy was by now well advanced, a condition Pete was more than happy with, physically, as in every other way. 'I think she is looking even more attractive than ever, but she just won't believe me,' he said. 'I reckon she's now more in proportion. I actually prefer Katie pregnant, because she's now so womanly and gorgeous; she just blows me away.'

Indeed, Pete was so excited at the prospect of impending fatherhood that he cancelled his forthcoming tour so that he could be present when his child was born. His newly resurgent musical career was one thing, but this was quite another, but he still felt bad about the fans.

'Peter Andre apologises that his tour will be rescheduled to start in November 2005,' a spokesman explained. 'Peter has been out to LA to work on some new music and the good news is he will be travelling back to

LA to record new tracks over the next few weeks, which he promises to perform on tour in November. He is also in talks with various record companies and a new single is planned in the coming months. With Peter and Katie recently announcing the exciting news, he is taking his family commitments seriously and wants to make sure he is at the birth.'

And then there was the wedding to plan. Katie and Pete wanted to invite a selection of their friends from the jungle, especially Kerry, with whom Katie had formed a bond, and friend Charlotte Church was to be another invitee. Indeed, Kerry was to be a bridesmaid.

'I was quite shocked when she asked me as I never thought she would,' said Kerry in an interview with *OK!* magazine. 'But, when I look back, I was there when they had their first kiss and I did egg on their romance – not that they needed much egging on.'

The ceremony was clearly going to be lavish, and they could certainly afford it: Katie appeared at No. 8 in the *Sunday Times* Rich List of Young Model Millionaires in April 2005. It was estimated she'd earned a good £5 million since leaving the jungle, and she hadn't been doing badly before that, either.

'She has a natural ability to turn her relentless exposure into hard cash,' said Philip Beresford, compiler of the Rich List. 'She showed she has a shrewd head for business by setting up Jordan Trading Limited in 2003 and, in its first year alone, sales topped £367,000. That showed her determination to keep sales of her image on calendars, magazines and merchandising under control.'

Certainly, the world was beginning to wake up to the fact that Katie was far more than just a pretty face. For a start, there was the small fortune she's built up, and she was still only, at this stage, 26. And then there was what was now being referred to as the 'rebranding' – the change in her image from glamour girl to someone other women could relate to.

Although she had advisers, Katie herself was behind a lot of it, realising that her shelf-life as a model would have been a short one, whereas, as a more mainstream celebrity, she still had the potential for decades of gain to come.

Nor did the relationship with Pete hurt. It was widely accepted that, career-wise, he needed her far more than she needed him, and yet still the burgeoning romance simply added to her allure. Katie had had to endure, rather publicly, some very bad behaviour from some of the men in her life, and so for the public to see her in a happy relationship was both heartening for her fans who were unlucky in love, and cheering for the world in general, watching someone who'd had a raw deal blossoming in front of their very eyes. The Danes and Dwights in her life were now all but forgotten as she concentrated on building up a new life with the man she was shortly to wed.

That business nous came out again when *OK!* magazine paid the duo £1.75 million for the rights to the wedding pictures, easily the highest price paid for a celebrity wedding so far. The deal was dependent on no wedding pictures appearing elsewhere, and so the couple's management hired a team of ex-SAS soldiers and intelligence officers to make sure everything went off without a hitch. And there was no doubt that quite a spectacle was to be laid on: Katie and Pete were not known for particularly subtle tastes and fans were hoping for an extravaganza. They would not be disappointed.

It was a measure of just how popular they were that the amount paid to cover their wedding was nearly double that of Catherine Zeta-Jones and Michael Douglas, a few years earlier – even the brightest stars in the Hollywood A-list were no match for Peter Andre and Katie Price. As for the Beckhams, their own wedding had been bought up some years previously for just £1 million, and given the rivalry between Katie and Victoria, still there despite Katie's placatory remarks, Katie could be forgiven for feeling a little gleeful. The many people who had never taken her seriously were certainly being called on to do so now.

But, before any of that could come to fruition, their next child was due to arrive. By now, Katie and Pete knew that it would be a boy and had taken numerous tests to make sure that everything was as it should be, health-wise, but, of course, they couldn't help but worry that the new arrival would have as many problems as Harvey. That was one reason they'd taken a long time to announce Katie's pregnancy, and would be a constant issue for both of them right up until the child was born.

'Having the scan come back clear in February was a relief,' said a pensive Katie to the *Mirror*, as the couple revealed the full extent of the tests she'd had to take. 'But everything looked fine with Harvey too at that stage, so we won't know 100 per cent until the baby is born. So, while it was a relief because it looked normal, I can't properly accept it yet until the baby arrives. But, if I did have another child with Harvey's problems again, I am prepared for it now because the constant care has become such a part of my life. In fact, I would probably find it difficult with a child that is normal because I'm so used to the routine.'

It was certainly not an easy life looking after her disabled son, even with Pete on hand to help. Harvey was only three, but weighed five stone; he could barely see and was feared to be autistic, but that was just a few of the many conditions he suffered from. Katie might have made a great deal of her life in other ways, but nothing shielded her from the reality of looking after a child who would always need care. It had made her the spokesman for other disabled children, for, as much as her fame might have made her rich, she was also using it to draw attention to the problems other children and their parents shared. It was an exhausting life and she was determined to highlight to the world just how much work and worry it involved.

'People see me pushing Harvey around the shops and stare at me, but they have no idea what I go through,' she said. 'Every day Harvey has to have four kinds of medicine, and he will be on them for the rest of his life. I think people are quite ignorant about disabled children... until you have one of your own, you don't know what it's like. Or what a person feels and goes through. It really drains you mentally.'

It had certainly been a huge burden to bear. However, the fact that Pete was on the scene made a huge difference. This time around, it was to be a very different scenario: there were two parents, actively involved, both with each other and with the needs of the children. The importance of family to Pete cannot be emphasised enough; already he had been a superb father to Harvey and, now that he was to have a boy of his own, he was delirious with delight. Katie knew this, too.

'Last time round, I was very conscious of being on my own – which was hard – but, this time, I have Pete with me,' she said. 'He is very good with Harvey and already changes dirty nappies! We're really looking forward to the baby. I am definitely going for a natural birth. God, I'm certainly not too posh to push! Last time I went natural and I will this time.'

But she remained very aware of the problems faced by

her first child – and the people who had to look after handicapped children. Indeed, so concerned was Katie about the plight of other mothers who were in her position, except without the help and finances to lighten, albeit slightly, the load that she had become patron of The Caudwell Charity, an organisation which cared for very sick children. It brought out a far more serious side of her than most people ever had cause to suspect.

'There was no support for me when I had Harvey,' she recalled, talking of her plans to raise money for the charity, as well as to boost its profile simply by being on board. 'It was only by talking with other mums that I started to get help – there was no support from the NHS at all. I know what it's like to sit at home worrying about what will happen tomorrow; that's why I wanted to get involved in the charity. I've always wanted to swim with sharks and go wing-walking! So that's what I'm planning to do once the baby is born, hopefully to raise money for the charity.

'I have this profile so I might as well use that to help other people. What's the point of it all otherwise?'

This, too, was a world away from her old image: Katie Price heading up a charity was nothing like Jordan falling out of a nightclub. Quite apart from anything else, the events of the past few years had forced her to become far more mature.

There had been some confusion about the due date: Katie and Pete had not announced her pregnancy for five months, owing to concerns about the health of the baby, and seemed themselves at some stage to have got their timing wrong. In the event, the new arrival appeared about a month before he was expected, on 13 June 2005. Katie had publicly stated her desire to have the child naturally, but, in the event, complications in the pregnancy meant she had to have a Caesarean after all. She gave birth at the private Portland Hospital in central London and a beaming Pete appeared afterwards to confirm that all was well.

'Katie and I are so happy to say we had a baby boy at three minutes past ten this morning,' he told assembled photographers. 'He's beautiful and healthy and he does look like me, I have to tell you that. We were a bit scared because it wasn't due for another three to four weeks and Katie had a few complications last night, so the doctor suggested she had a Caesarean this morning.'

But that was as nothing compared to their worries about how the baby was going to be – as Katie had said, no one realised that Harvey would have problems until after he was born. In the event, however, the latest addition to the family proved to be absolutely fine.

Pete, the ecstatic father, had been present throughout and was now showing all the signs of being a deliriously happy newborn's dad. He was asked how Katie was doing. 'She's great, a really brave girl,' he replied. 'I'm a bit nervous and very proud, and we are the happiest people in the world, I swear to God. I was more emotional than she was at the birth. One thing I want to say is that no words can explain what you feel at that moment. People always say, "You'll never understand," but now I know.

'He looks just like me. That might disappoint some people but it makes me very happy.'

Clearly, the birth of his first child had changed his life. Fatherhood is an event that makes a profound impression on any man, but for Pete, with his Cypriot background, it mattered a huge amount. It also added a layer that had not been there before. He had been a lad in his time, taking full advantage of the many opportunities out there for a single young man who is also a successful pop star, but this was something different. Now he had a child (two, actually, including Harvey). For him, the whole experience was profound.

Mother and child were well; they stayed in the hospital for a further five days until both were allowed home. A couple of days after that, the name of the new child was announced: it was to be Junior. And now everyone really could relax. Katie had been called upon to be very brave for the last time, but now she had been rewarded with a child that was perfectly happy, with no special needs and no concerns about special care. It was a golden period in the relationship, with a healthy child and a wedding just round the corner: the couple couldn't have been happier, and it showed.

It was to be some time before cracks began to show in the relationship – indeed, they would go on to have another child – and Pete was probably harking back to this period when he wrote of his sadness at the break-up of a relationship several years on.

Katie, meanwhile, lost no time in getting herself back in shape: she had been 8 stone 2lb before her pregnancy and 10 stone 3lb at the height of it. It was her job to look good (although it often happened that people who saw her in the flesh commented how tiny she was, with the obvious exception of her chest) and she was determined to turn this round immediately. Apart from anything else, the wedding was only a few months away, after all, and she certainly wanted to look good for that.

Katie tackled her figure with her usual industriousness and enthusiasm. She knew what she wanted – to be super-slim again – and that was what she would be. In less than a month, she managed to lose a stone, but there was still a way to go.

'Now I'm nine stone two pounds, so I've got a stone to go,' she said at the time. 'I'll do it, though. Now I've got a professional trainer, and I'm going to work out and eat all the right foods. I'm making a fitness video and I'm going to get fit the right way.'

There it was again – that combination of personal self-discipline and business nous. If Katie was going to lose weight, then she would document that battle and profit from it financially, as well as physically. She saw opportunity everywhere and was never slow to act. And she went on to achieve her goals, losing all the weight she wanted to and appearing radiant on the big day itself too.

She was building her empire up in other ways, too, launching a range of lingerie in 2006 called 'Katie Price' to sell through Asda, which prompted prurient comments from some quarters, but was clearly an obvious step for her to take. For someone whose physique was commented on as much as hers, why not launch a line such as this? It went on to sell well, too, silencing the doubters. People might have questioned Katie's taste, but there was no arguing with the growing amount of cash in the bank.

And she was thinking about other possibilities, too. There was also talk of a range of clothes for bigger tots, something else she'd had to deal with on a personal basis, due to the disabilities of her eldest child.

'I'm thinking about launching a range of kids' clothes for larger children,' said Katie. 'Harvey is really hard to buy for because he needs stuff for twelve-year-olds. The problem is, a lot of it isn't suitable for him, so I have to do a lot of hunting around. We're not the only family with this problem, which is why I'd like to have a go at designing some clothes. I think it's something that could really take off.'

Indeed, at that point, everything that Katie and Pete touched seemed to turn to gold. Now there were two websites: one for Katie Price and the other for Jordan, both run by her brother, Danny. Pete had just the one website, but his career was doing far better than anyone expected, even after the initial surge in sales when he came out of the jungle. He had not disappeared from view, as so many of the more jaundiced observers of the celebrity scene had forecast he would; if anything, interest in him continued to grow as it did in Katie. Together, they were far greater than the sum of their parts.

And both of them were happy. It was a sign of her contentment with life, in many ways, that made Katie so able to think about possibilities and to plan ahead. She and Pete had been together for more than a year now and the two of them appeared to be settling down into long-term happiness. There was none of the public aggression and aggro that she'd experienced in previous relationships, while Pete had never looked so comfortable as he did now, in the role of doting dad. He was a doting partner, as well – utterly besotted with the beautiful Katie, and giving every indication of a man who had come home at last. The two of them adored each other, that much was clear, and now they had a child together and were about to wed. Together, they had proved the doubters wrong and were both ready to take the next step.

And so the couple settled down with two children, Harvey and Junior, and for a time, matters couldn't have been better. A great deal of this must be laid at Pete's door:

he had risen to the occasion in a way that even his greatest admirers couldn't have foretold. And, in doing so, he was proving a catch to any woman, let alone one who had had such a rough time of it in the past.

Katie realised this. 'Pete's a really good hands-on dad,' she remarked. 'He treats both Junior and Harvey the same, which is important. If any guy wouldn't accept Harvey, they can forget being with me. He's part of me, and that's it. We'll have more kids, but I want to enjoy Junior first – I don't want him to be a year old and me pregnant with another one; it's too stressful. I want to carry on with my career for a few years first. There's no rush, but we will be having lots of kids. How many more? It depends how big a car they design!'

They were indeed to go on to have another child, and for some years to come, experienced great happiness together. But, for now, something else was on their minds: looming up in the near distance was the next Katie and Pete extravaganza, and what a show this would turn out to be. The two of them were about to get married – and the spectacle was to remain in the minds of observers for years to come.

CHAPTER EIGHT
WEDDING BELLE

As the year moved into summer, there was increasing speculation about the wedding itself. It was clear it was going to be a show stopper, but, even so, rumours emanating from the bridal camp made it clear that something big was on the cards. The details were to be kept a secret until the day itself, but that couldn't prevent increasingly wild speculation. Katie and Pete looked on with a mixture of amusement and bemusement as story after counter-story made their way into the public's imagination.

Of course, the greatest curiosity surrounded the dress. No one was quite certain who was making it (it was to be a designer also favoured by Nancy Dell'Olio, with whom Katie shared a certain sartorial style), or what it would really be like. There was one rumour to the effect that Katie was going to try to smash the world record for trains, currently set at 2,545 feet in a 2002 Dutch ceremony.

'Jordan looks amazing in the dress,' said one source, who claimed to have seen it. 'No one will believe how huge it is until they see it. She wanted her special day to be remembered by everyone and she has certainly made sure of that. The dress really is something else, but not in a tacky way; she just wanted to do something different. Jordan is going to need a lot of bridesmaids to help carry her train on the day. It will steal the show and everyone will remember it for years to come.'

That report ultimately turned out not to be true, although Katie herself had something to say about how she would be appearing at the ceremony: 'You might see some flesh on show – but not cellulite.'

Then it emerged that a horse-drawn carriage was to feature, too. It had been confirmed that the wedding was to be at Highclere Castle, near Newbury, Berks, and not in the Scottish highlands, as had originally been thought to be the case, and the bride and groom were not holding back.

'The horse-drawn carriage will be used to take them along the mile-long drive,' said another friend. 'They will sit in it, lording it up like a prince and a princess. Katie is horse-mad anyway, as she likes to ride out often. She wanted the animals to play a big part in the wedding.'

In fact, this particular report was true: the wedding was

to have a Cinderella theme, and so this was the pumpkin that turned into a glass coach.

With only a month to go before the wedding itself, there was intense concern when Harvey had to spend some time in Great Ormond Street Hospital for Children, leading to concerns that the ceremony might have to be postponed. In the event, however, Katie and Pete decided to go ahead. Harvey's health was such that there would never be a time when he was certain to be well and, anyway, the preparations were at an advanced stage. Huge logistical problems would have been created had the date for the ceremony been pushed back.

The invitations had already gone out: they were posted in a silver-and-white jewellery box and printed on a silver-and-white crepe paper scroll that read:

> Peter Andre and Katie Price request the pleasure
> of your company at their marriage on Saturday,
> 10 September 2005. Guests arrival at 3.15pm.
> Wedding ceremony 4pm at Highclere Castle,
> Newbury, Berkshire.

Guests were also informed that they would be filmed during the course of the proceedings.

On the whole, everyone felt it was right to go ahead, not least because Katie's mother advised it. It was the right decision to take; it also showed the closeness of the bond between Katie and Amy. When her marriage to Pete broke down, three-and-a-half years on, it was her mother in whom Katie confided and who spoke out in her support.

'Kate has always listened to her mum and really appreciated her stepping in to save the day,' said a friend. 'There have been so many people working on this wedding it would be a crying shame to cancel it. Peter told Kate he understood if she postponed it. Harvey has a growth hormone deficiency and it could end up affecting his heart. He's still poorly, but in the best possible hands.'

Katie was visibly distressed by events, however, and was seen in tears as she jetted off for a short trip to Cyprus to see Pete's parents in the run-up to the big day. This was not her usual style – life had toughened her up – and so to see the stress getting to her was proof indeed of the toll it was taking.

There was also some upset about what had been appearing in the press in the build-up to the wedding. A sneering tone was evident in some quarters, with false reports that the wedding cake would be modelled on the shape of the bride's chest, as well as claims that various celebrities, including Charlotte Church, were turning their invitations down. It turned out that Katie was miffed about the 'longest train' story, too. Matters got so bad that Katie's spokeswoman decided to put it straight, announcing, 'The do won't be tacky. Kate is not having a "boob cake". People have been saying she is going to have a cake in the shape of a pair of boobs. Peter and Kate think it's really horrible to say things like this when they are looking forward to their dream day. People just need to be a bit nicer. It's going to be an amazing day for them and they are really excited. The people they really wanted to come who cannot come have sent Kate and Peter really lovely letters. [Charlotte Church] wrote a really lovely letter. Kate and Charlotte are good friends.'

But the strain really was taking its toll. There were reports of another bust-up with Javine – the two didn't appear to be able to resist sniping at one another

Besides, none of this really mattered in light of what was about to take place. The long-awaited marriage, the outcome of all that flirtation in the jungle, really was about to happen. And it was, in fact, quite a day for weddings: Katie and Pete's nuptials were scheduled for the same day as three other big dos: Tom Parker Bowles and Sara Buys, Jodie Kidd and Aiden Butler, and Derek Draper and Kate Garraway. But none was quite like Katie's and Pete's, which, as ever, was in a league of its own.

No wedding is complete without a family row, and some members of Katie's extended family duly obliged. Her aunt Renee Ansell was not on the guest list and took exception to being left out. 'We haven't been invited because she would rather have so-called celebrities there than her family,' she told the *Mirror*. 'She was a good girl, but she's changed. It's all about money and I suppose to get this magazine deal she needs to fill the wedding with celebrities, not ordinary people. We wouldn't look good in the pictures.

'I met him [Pete] at a family birthday party last year and I found him charming. He seemed really nice, but I think Katie might have changed him. That day was the last time I saw her and she never even spoke to me.'

Katie's first boyfriend, Gary Bolingbroke, also felt the need to speak out. 'One hundred per cent guaranteed there will be a ruckus,' said the electrician, who had dated Katie in her teens. 'It's that family, there is no way there won't be some trouble. I would never have married her, but, if I had, it wouldn't have been a big, showy wedding like this.'

Chances are Katie would never have married him either, of course.

And, when her real big day finally arrived, she was clearly loving every minute of it. Everything had been planned down to the last detail. Both bride and groom were careful not to be photographed, with security cordons, security guards and the police keeping fans and photographers at bay. Celebrity guests, including Vanessa Feltz and Jennifer Ellison, turned up, along with Jennie Bond, Lord Brocket, Paul Gascoigne, Wayne Rooney, Coleen McLoughlin, Ian Wright, Dean Gaffney and Michael Greco. Alongside Kerry as bridesmaid was Girls Aloud singer Sarah Harding, while guests were serenaded by *The X Factor*'s Rowetta.

And the event certainly lived up to expectations. A civil ceremony was held in the library of Highclere Castle, followed by a blessing in the Secret Garden. Katie was dressed in a pink tulle and satin gown studded with pink crystals, designed by Isabell Kristensen, with a 7-metre train (not quite so long as the rumoured one, but still pretty impressive) and topped off with a foot-high pink tiara. Pete was wearing an ivory suit by the same designer, made of Venetian wool, with a glittering waistcoat studded with Swarovski crystals. Whatever you thought of their taste, the couple certainly stood out: the focal point of attention in the middle of a crowd and a location that had gone totally over the top.

The reception was held in a marquee that was also decorated in pink and full of bay trees adorned with pink feathers and crystals, a 10-foot chandelier plus two thrones, decked out in lilac, and pink flowers. Katie did indeed arrive in a glass coach, or rather a pink-pumpkin version, while guests dined on foie gras and lobster served by waiters who were also singing opera.

There were, of course, moments of drama. One guest reported the following: 'Jordan's stepfather Paul made a speech and mentioned Kate's real dad,' he said. 'She immediately jumped up, grabbed the microphone and said, "Where are you?" and Ray stood up at the back table.

'She was shocked to see him sitting so far away from her other family members and yelled, "You should be at the front table. Whoever put you at the back table, I'm going to bollock them!" She was not happy about it at all. It definitely took some of the shine off her big day.'

And Katie was uncharacteristically tense. 'I thought I was going to have a panic attack just before I walked down the aisle,' she admitted. 'I think it was because I was being filmed and everyone was staring. I had no doubt I was going to marry Pete, but I didn't know if I was going to faint first. I don't normally get nervous, but that day I was so overwhelmed.' In the event, she carried it off perfectly, but she herself clearly felt at one stage that it was a case of touch and go.

There had also nearly been an accident before the service even began. 'On the way to the castle, the carriage crashed into a bush and I really thought it was going to tip over and throw me out,' said Katie. 'It took half the side of the carriage off. I actually had a sparkly pink tutu on in the carriage because my dress was too big to fit inside it.' Again, all was well, and the carriage got to the castle safely. Once in situ, Katie swapped her tutu for her voluptuous gown and the proceedings really began.

To everyone's relief, Harvey was well enough to attend, and was walked up the aisle by the bridesmaids, giving great joy to the attending family. And the spectacle was not just photographed by *OK!* – the duo had embarked on their second reality-television series together, this time called *Jordan & Peter: Marriage & Mayhem*, which was to show the wedding in all its full glory. Intended to be screened just over a week after the event, viewers were also allowed in behind the scenes of the pregnancy as well as the wedding, as the six-part series actually started filming around the time that Katie discovered she was pregnant. Viewers were finally to see all.

Like so many young couples, however, marriage proper didn't really begin until the next day. 'I was too knackered,' revealed Katie to an interviewer shortly afterwards, a session at which Pete was also present. 'And so was he. Yes, you were knackered! Shut up! We didn't have sex, but we were so hungry we had a crisp sandwich in bed. I ate hardly anything on the day, I was so busy. I'd been so looking forward to all this food and, when it got there, I was too busy talking and looking around to eat anything. I can't wait to see it again on the telly. But we did consummate the marriage on the Sunday morning.'

She was also ecstatic about the fact that they woke up the next morning as husband and wife. Asked how it felt, she replied, 'Amazing. We opened our eyes and there were balloons and presents everywhere and my wedding dress on the floor. All the way home we were going, "We're married, we're married!" I wish we'd had a big "Just Married" sticker to put on the car.'

Despite the wedding taking place in the public eye and the fact that this was one of the most famous couples in Britain, they were still primarily a young couple in love, after all. And their delight in their new domestic set-up mirrored vast numbers of other young couples throughout the land.

In all, the wedding, the magazine deal and the television series were deemed to be a great success, but a measure of the strange world in which Katie and Pete now lived came about a week after the wedding, when Katie called the police in order to stop a photographer taking pictures of her in a hair salon. It was a slightly bizarre incident, although no stranger than so much else that was now part of the couple's life.

It started when the Sussex Police received a call from a woman who said she was being followed by 'a strange man'.

'We didn't know who it was,' said a spokeswoman. 'The emergency call came in saying, "We are being followed by a strange man and my two young children are with me." Two response vehicles were sent to the scene, as we would do in those circumstances, and they were there very quickly.

'On arrival, we established that the woman in question was actually Katie Price and that the man was a photographer, and we took details and gave out advice before Ms Price made her way off.'

Whether or not the photographer was a real threat was immaterial. The event confirmed Katie and Pete were now living life completely in the public eye, with every move they made recorded by cameras, whether it was through their magazine deals or reality television. Being confronted with slightly bizarre behaviour might be deeply worrying, although the fact was that the man almost certainly just wanted to take a few pictures. The lives of the newly-weds were still of fascination to everyone else.

But they were married now, and loving every minute of it. And again, like so many more 'normal' couples, the vows they had taken had had a profound effect. 'I didn't expect this, but I think it feels different,' said Katie. 'I feel that extra commitment. Like we can't be kids, either. I say to Pete, "Well, if we're going to break up, you're going to have to divorce me." It all sounds really grown-up.'

Those were, alas, prophetic words: when the marriage finally fell apart, it was indeed Pete who initiated proceedings. At the time, however, this was all just talk.

The ultimate split was particularly sad, because now Katie revealed that, in actual fact, she'd had a crush on her new husband for years. Now that she was married to Pete, she was asked whom she had wanted to marry when she was growing up.

'Pete!' she replied. 'Well, I had a big crush on him years ago when I saw his "Mysterious Girl" video, but I never dreamed for one minute I'd marry him, or even meet him. When I did *I'm A Celebrity*... and they told me, "Peter Andre's on the show," I did think back and remember that six-pack. He was my type then, and he still is now. In Pete,

I've found my soul mate – he's everything I could ever want. We are so close, we do everything together and I can't imagine not being with him. And the sex is great.'

Now that it was all done and dusted, the pictures taken, and the need for absolute silence on the matter eradicated, Katie finally felt that she could answer some of the criticisms of the day that had been made public in the run-up to it, and beyond. And she couldn't resist having a go at the people who had been rather snooty about the wedding.

'I knew people were going to slate it anyway, whatever we did – and they did,' she said. 'But we, and the people there, know what a wicked day it was, so that's all that matters. There were so many stories – as if we were going to have a cake like my tits. It was our wedding; it's a serious thing. A bloody tit cake! That's enough to put anyone off eating.'

Her bemusement at the idea was also proof that she and Pete had taken the proceedings mightily seriously: the wedding might have been flamboyant, but they absolutely did not want to promote tackiness. And, of course, they had ended up having a spectacularly fine day.

And, finally, Katie was adamant about what was important – and that was to remain absolutely faithful to her new husband and he to her. 'Once a cheater, always a cheater,' she explained. 'If Pete cheated, I wouldn't take him back. Life is too short and, if someone cheats on you, they aren't showing you respect and that's something everyone deserves. Whether I've got a kid with him or not, if he cheats, he's out.'

In the event, he didn't, but sadly the marriage ended anyway. Back then, however, in the aftermath of the ceremony, the two of them sounded like love-struck young teenagers, certain they would be together forever. Alas, it was to turn out very differently.

After a honeymoon in the Maldives, it was back to business. Katie had just become the face of the Young Attitude lingerie range and turned up at the launch at Debenhams wearing the same tutu she had worn on the drive of Highclere Castle on her wedding day. Her predecessors in the role had either been, or were about to be married to Rod Stewart: Rachel Hunter and Penny Lancaster. Michelle Mone, who created the range for larger-busted women, scored something of a coup. A huge crowd turned out to the launch ('Who knows who Penny Lancaster is?' asked Katie), and she was making it clear that, despite the marriage, it was absolutely business as usual.

The designer herself appeared to be delighted by the deal. 'I am really excited that we have signed Katie,' she said. 'Her personality reflects what Young Attitude stands for – sexy, fun and outgoing, and Katie is definitely the woman with the right attitude.'

Katie too seemed thrilled. 'I am over the moon to be chosen as the face of Young Attitude,' she said.

Later, during the launch, she told one reporter, 'Oh yes, I love him to bits and I hope it lasts forever, but, if it doesn't, it doesn't. I don't need a man. Everything I've got, I've paid for. No disrespect to those who marry a rich guy and live off him, but I could never do that. I've worked since I was twelve and, since I was fifteen, I've stuck my boobs out and got on with it.'

She was similarly dismissive of anyone who had criticised the wedding, saying, 'It was about Pete and I. I wanted a girlie dream. When I was a little girl, my mother bought me all the Cinderella books but I never thought that I would be able to afford to drive in a coach like that with all the horses, and those we didn't invite and anyone who thinks my dress was naff is bad-mouthing one of our best designers.'

Certainly, whatever the carpers had to say about it, Katie's influence could not be underestimated. In the wake of the wedding, sales of similar meringue pink wedding dresses shot up.

'I'm quite surprised at how well this style has taken off,' admitted Kahlua Cameron of Capri Skies, an upmarket shop in Glasgow. 'Ever since Jordan's wedding, most of our clients head straight for our full-skirted dresses when they come through our doors and, the minute they try on the dress, they fall in love all over again.'

Katie's influence on others was felt again when she came top of a poll to find the body most women want:

she herself, ironically, was now considering a breast reduction. She was also extremely open to the thought of plastic surgery, saying, 'I would never want to grow old gracefully. When I'm old I'd want to still look like I do in my twenties.

'I'm sure there will be some new inventions to help me look younger as well, you just don't know what will be around by then. You never know, they might even have invented a way of not ageing by then. But I tell you something now, you will never, ever see me with grey hair. I will dye it immediately if I go grey.'

Given that she was already no stranger to the surgeon's knife, it was perhaps no surprise that she was prepared to go further there, too.

'I will probably have plastic surgery on my face too,' she continued. 'I definitely wouldn't go for everything at the same time, but, if I was starting to not like the way I was looking, I would do something about it. I'd definitely do Botox again, and, if I was getting lines round my eyes, I'd do something about it. I'm always looking at what's wrong with me and thinking about what I can do better.'

Her new husband too was prepared to fight to hold back the years, although not with quite the same intensity as his wife.

'I'd quite like to grow old naturally, but I'm willing to try things,' he said. 'I had Botox recently and it's amazing. It felt like needles of acid when it was being done, but the results are fantastic. It's not like my forehead's totally numb or anything, it's just all the lines have disappeared.'

But the more serious side of life was never far away. Just two months after the wedding, Harvey was back in Great Ormond Street Hospital, his mother as concerned as ever.

'Kate has been worried sick about Harvey,' said a friend of the couple. 'He's very poorly and was in hospital for a few days having two operations. The growth hormone problem means there can be a lot of pressure at times on Harvey's heart and it is a constant worry for the family. Kate stayed at the hospital with him and Pete went to visit too. Obviously they have their baby Junior to look after as well, so it has been a bit of a nightmare.

'But Kate takes great comfort in knowing Harvey is in the best possible hands at Great Ormond Street. He's doing OK now and is back at home, recovering. He's had lots of problems and Kate and Pete are naturally very concerned, but they have grown used to having to manage with all his medical troubles and they are strong as a couple.'

As the year drew to a close, rather mystifyingly Katie was dropped as the face of Young Attitude.

'We have no plans to use Jordan again, but we don't know yet who is going to take over Young Attitude,' announced Michelle Mone. 'We've just got to see what our customers want and what they would like. Young Attitude is a really sophisticated brand; it's meant to be at a high end of the market. We've got quite a lot of names in the running at the moment. She's got to be young, fresh, sophisticated and have a good personality, as well as having big boobs.'

In some quarters, there had been doubts as to whether Katie was quite the right person to front the campaign, but it seemed something quite different was really at play here. It must be said, Michelle had caused controversy, and thus publicity; in previous years, she first hired Penny Lancaster to model her Ultimo range and then dropped her in favour of Rachel Hunter, creating a huge row at the time. It seems likely something similar might have happened here.

But Katie had so many other projects going on, it was unlikely to have concerned her too greatly. Next up was her fitness DVD, *The Jordan Workout* (released in December 2005), and she was happy to go into the usual graphic detail about her likes and how it was best to work out.

'A lot of people say sex is the best way to get fit, but I disagree,' she began. 'I work up a much better sweat during my workout than in bed with Pete. I've tried to get him to give my regime a try, but he prefers boxing and weight training to squatting and lunging. Peter has his own ideas about the best way for us to work out together and I'm not complaining, but I rely on my own regime to make sure I hit the spot, fitness-wise. He appreciates the figure I have as a result of my training. Pete is always telling me not to lose any more weight. He likes a woman to look like a woman.'

Indeed, while very slim herself, Katie professed no fondness for the size-zero girls. 'They look rank,' she said. 'They have taken dieting a step too far – you could play a tune on their ribs. Men don't find that look sexy at all. I never want to be like that. I am naturally slim, but I haven't got bones poking through – I just look nice and toned.'

As she said, she had always been naturally slim, but, like so many other women, she now found that she had to work harder to maintain her physique. 'I've never had to exercise before,' she said. 'I used to eat what I wanted, when I wanted.

'I was the laziest person you'd ever met and would always be eating junk food – Chinese, pizza and curry were my favourite meals. All I worried about was having my hair and nails done. But Peter is really into fitness, so we had a gym built in our house. There is a sun-bed in it and, although I always seem to be able to find time for the sun-bed, I never have time for a workout.'

But it was the birth of Junior that had changed all that. Not only had Katie put on two stone while carrying the child but she had to lose the weight very quickly to look her best when she got married.

'Every girl wants to look her best on her wedding day,' she said. 'I'm no exception so I decided to combine getting trim with making a workout video. That way it meant I had to stick to it. Once I had the challenge of getting fit after having a baby, I thought it was an ideal opportunity to give people a real workout, one they could see actually worked.'

Of course, it was a good commercial opportunity, too, but Katie's very public image meant that her fans could see that the new regime actually did work.

'Everyone saw pictures of me during my pregnancy and after the birth so they could see what a huge difference the workout made,' she explained. 'This workout is for everyone and I am the proof that it works. I weighed more than 10 stone after I had my baby and now, at 8 stone, I'm the smallest I have ever been.'

In fact, almost worryingly so. For, while Katie was at that stage looking happy and healthy, she was the sort of person who lost weight dramatically when she was under stress and, in the days following the final breakdown of her marriage, she was to appear quite gaunt. But all that was in the future – for now.

CHAPTER NINE
JORDAN, THE MOVIE

The New Year, 2006, kicked off as it meant to go on: with a bang. Katie and Peter were now so much a part of the landscape that there was some speculation a film might be made of Katie's life. And it had been the most extraordinary story to date. Many people who start their lives as glamour models end up coming across as victims, but not in this case. Setbacks she might have had, but rarely in the world has there been a person less of a victim than Katie. Nor, it was becoming increasingly clear, was she doomed to have the short shelf-life of most glamour models. She'd already been on the scene for nearly a decade, and there she most definitely intended to stay.

Why not a film? Katie modestly declined the lead role, but indicated she might be tempted by a walk-on part. 'My next thing is to do a film,' she explained in a radio interview. 'I'm trying to find people now like directors and that who want to do it. I'll probably get someone to play me and then I'll make an appearance in it.'

At the time of writing, plans have got no further, but her life has become even more eventful since then.

And everything the two of them said or did made the news. They seemed to have a genius for turning every element of their lives into fodder for an adoring public: right down to the Christmas presents. Pete had given Katie a year's worth of flying lessons as a gift, which prompted another unusual wish. 'I want a helicopter,' Katie declared. 'I'm going to learn how to fly because I hate sitting in traffic.' The colour of this new toy, she said, would be pink.

Now that Katie was presenting herself as Katie, rather than Jordan, and now that she was a respectable married woman, there were increasing signs that she wanted to put her glamour-girl past behind her. But, being Katie, she couldn't quite do so without a bit of a song and a dance. And so there was yet more merriment when she decided that she now wanted a breast reduction, and had plans for the silicone implants she would no longer need. 'I'm having them reduced because I want them a bit more pert,' she explained. 'I've had them eight years now. So it's time for a new pair and I'll sell this lot on eBay.'

And why not? Katie was showing herself to be so adept at making money that she probably could have flogged the implants off for a healthy sum if she'd tried (in the end, she didn't). This was a woman who knew how to turn her life into cash.

'I am definitely a good businesswoman,' she said firmly. 'Definitely. Never underestimate the Pricey! I'm not going to tell you how or give you details, because I don't want to give my secret away. But I have learned the hard way and I know what people want. I know what works, and I know what sells.'

She was careful, too. Despite all the flamboyance, Katie did not push the boat out when she could not afford to do so, and had been building up her fortune and her career solidly right from the start. Her brother Daniel helped: he did her bookkeeping and accounts, while his sister simply went out and earned even more.

'I like to keep my money matters in the family,' explained Katie. 'I left school at sixteen and at seventeen I worked in a care home and then started to train as a nurse. I took home £90 and I managed to run my Mini, keep my horse and go out at weekends. Then I got my big break as a Page 3 girl. Deep down, I always knew that I would not end up having a nine-to-five job. Whatever your chosen field, you have to work hard – and work from the bottom up.'

Indeed, she was full of excellent advice for people who were starting out. 'Whatever your profession, know it inside out and be prepared to start on the ground floor,' she said. 'My talent is knowing what I want and never taking "No" for an answer. I always set out my goals and then work out how I am going to achieve them. I don't believe in failure. I haven't got a mortgage and I don't owe anything on credit. Cars are my biggest passion... and horses. I have just sold my Ferrari and want to buy a McLaren and another Range Rover.'

Not exactly the thoughts of a bimbo. One photographer who had worked with her in the early days provided an insight into the real Katie: he thought she was a pretty good businesswoman, too. 'One minute she seems hopelessly ditzy, quite capable of taking a pair of scissors to a £350 designer skirt if she doesn't like the length of it,' he said. 'Then she shocks you with some astute remark and you realise there's a very shrewd girl in there. I once heard her giving marching orders to a rich man who was making his interest in her obvious. But he was hardly intending to walk her down the aisle and she made her contempt for him – and how well she understood his assumptions about a girl like her – very clear.'

Katie herself once expressed her attitude to men like that in no uncertain terms. 'It's a pain,' she admitted, in an interview shortly after she started out. 'Too many men think the only thing a glamour model is interested in is money. They're always telling me how much of it they've got, and they do this with it and that with it. I'm not interested. I've got my own money.'

Indeed, it was noteworthy that, when she did pick a

husband, although he certainly wasn't poor, he didn't have a higher financial status than his wife. Katie, as was obvious to all, was clearly the dominant partner in the relationship – until, of course, she pushed him too far.

The money had a downside too, though, and, in May 2006, there were reports that a gang of criminals had been planning to kidnap one of the children for a £1 million ransom demand. The police were called and security around the family stepped up: it made Katie's concern about being followed to the hairdressers understandable. But the plot was foiled before anything more took place.

'Obviously Katie's main concern is for her kids,' said a friend. 'She's used to being in the limelight and knows the risks which that brings, particularly when her fortune has been so widely discussed. She has been targeted by burglars in the past. But this is different – it's a sinister turn because it puts the boys at risk. Katie is working closely with police to do everything in her power to keep them safe.'

Unpleasant as it was, it was a matter to be dealt with and, utterly pragmatic, Katie and Pete did indeed deal with it. And, say what you like about Katie, she was her own person in a way most celebrities couldn't even dream of. Everything about her was unique, despite the efforts of many would-be imitators, right down to what she wore.

'I design, make or customise my clothes,' she declared at

one point. 'I do it myself on my sewing machine. I do the same with Harvey's clothes. I buy from boutiques in Brighton, where I live. I like Guess and Roberto Cavalli dresses and Isabell Kristensen, who made my wedding dress.' As she so often pointed out, hers was not a figure that was easy to dress: a tiny frame with large breasts, and so, even when she did buy ready-to-wear outfits, adjustments constantly had to be made. Another favoured designer was Versace, but, as with Cavalli, Katie couldn't fit into the clothes snugly because her figure was so unusual. And, of course, there was the pragmatic side to her. Those designers cost a lot of money, and, unlike her rival Victoria Beckham, this was money she was not prepared to pay.

However, the flamboyant aspect was only half the story. Katie and Pete were not out every night, and, in those early days, they'd achieved some level of domestic bliss. On one occasion, she described a night in, customising again, and the couple practically sounded like Darby and Joan, albeit with rather more flamboyant tastes.

'My mum had a sewing machine she used to make curtains with and, when she got a new one, she gave the old one to me,' she recalled. 'I started off my king horse rugs with it, but then I started the customising – customising my clothes. I still do that now; I make so many clothes from scratch. I make Harvey's clothes – little tracksuits and things.

'Me and Pete take it in turns to do the cooking, and my sewing machine's in the kitchen so he'll be there, chopping, and I'll be sewing. Sewing and sewing. I've got patterns cut out, all the fabric cut up just waiting. I can make a tracksuit for Harvey in forty minutes. I like making clothes for him, but with Junior... I think babies should be in babygros – cuddly and comfy. I have made them both matching tracksuits, though.'

It was a far cry from falling out of nightclubs in the glamour days. The unsuitable men were a thing of the past, for now marriage and babies were completely on her mind. And she'd found the right man, too.

On another occasion, Pete painted a similarly idyllic picture of their life together. Asked about the simple pleasures in life, he replied, 'Watching my children. I love seeing them happy and wondering what they're thinking. Children are incredibly moody. One minute they're laughing, the next they're crying; I love that about them. Being a parent has changed me. The world no longer revolves around me, it revolves around them and that would change anyone. I'm fortunate because I'd wanted children before I met Katie, and so I was ready for it and I practised with Harvey for two years before Junior came along.'

For all the happiness, though, a more serious side was never far behind. In February 2006, Katie revealed that she'd had post-natal depression after the birth of Junior and was forced to undergo a spell in The Priory, the health clinic much frequented by stars. It was a side to her that the public were not used to seeing: this was not the happy-go-lucky model they knew of old, but a more serious woman with a complex set of issues.

'I wanted to feel happy, but I did not,' she said. 'I was not bonding [with Junior]. He [Pete] stuck by me when I was a psycho-dragon. I can't believe how differently I feel now. I'm a lot happier and having fun.'

And that, really, summed up her life: the party girl with a dark side. However, while Pete was very supportive back then, in the early days of their marriage and when she had just given birth to his first child, he would become increasingly unable to deal with the 'psycho-dragon' aspect of his wife's personality in the future. For now, though, this was kept under wraps.

In other areas of her life, Katie was becoming accustomed to having the last laugh and the opportunity to do so came again with the April 2006 issue of *American Vogue*. The most powerful woman in fashion, no less, Anna Wintour, the fearsome editor of the journal, gave Katie her official seal of approval when she put her in the magazine's shape issue. If *American Vogue* had become a fan (or, more likely, understood that its readers adored her), then Katie had arrived, indeed.

'She certainly addresses the challenge of dressing someone with significant breasts,' said Sally Singer,

Vogue's fashion news/features director. 'Appearing in our shape issue, Katie Price's figure is today not that unusual; a lot of women are top-heavy with tiny bodies that aren't perfectly symmetrical because they've been surgically altered, and that's something that fashion designers now have to reckon with.' But why choose Katie? 'Her appeal is that she exists on so many different levels.'

The photographer for the shoot, during which Katie was far more covered up than usual, and wore understated Lanvin, rather than OTT pink, was David Bailey. Over the previous four decades, Bailey had photographed almost every beautiful woman in the Western world, but even he found this a new challenge. He was forced to keep shouting, 'Keep them down!' as Katie directed her greatest assets towards the camera's gaze.

The resulting photoshoot, however, portrayed her as never before. Demure, but undeniably beautiful was the result. Given her cartoonish physique, it is often forgotten that Katie would have been an incredibly striking woman, even had her breasts not been inflated to larger than life. It was a salutary reminder, to her as well as everyone else, that her career did not just have to centre on her cleavage; there were plenty of other elements to her that people wanted as well.

There was another ominous reminder, though, that Katie had another side. That spring, Pete launched his autobiography. His wife, however, was less than enthusiastic about it (perhaps understandably so, since she had been on the receiving end of some teasing remarks about how she never read books).

'I'm not interested in his book, I'm not even going to read it,' she declared. She might have been joking, but it didn't come across that way. Rather, it appeared that Katie was beginning to feel rather competitive with her husband, a feeling that would only grow over the coming months and years. One of the many factors that led to the split was this urge to compete, and, given that Katie had the higher profile and was the considerably more combative partner in the relationship, it was bound to grind away at Pete. Of course, eventually, it did.

Another hint that not everything was rosy in paradise came from Mala Burns, who had dated Pete on and off in the pre-Katie days. Katie had upset her badly by claiming that Pete had dated her only for cheap airline tickets (Mala was an air stewardess), and, when Pete attempted to invite Mala to the wedding, a huge row had taken place. Now Mala was determined to have her say. According to her, Pete had met her in secret before the wedding and, while no impropriety took place, he did complain about how difficult his life had become. '"You've no idea what my life's been like these last six months,"' she said he told her. '"It's been hell. Katie's so insecure and jealous. We nearly split up." It's like his life is no longer his own. Since meeting Jordan, he's become a different person. Jordan strikes me

156

as incredibly possessive ... I truly believe he's partly with her for the money and the fame. I think part of Pete does love Jordan, but I think he loves the money and fame just as much.'

In fact, she was almost certainly wrong: there was every indication that Pete loved his wife and was prepared to put up with the downside to be with her. But that did not mean the problems went away. Back then, though, the odd moment of marital disharmony was quickly laughed off. And the high spirits continued – one minute Kate was telling Madame Tussauds to create figures of her and Pete – 'I would let them have my wedding dress, as long as they looked after it, and Pete would let them have his suit' – and the next she was making plans for the couple to renew their vows in Disneyworld.

'It'll be totally different from our wedding,' she declared. 'I don't want the stress of table plans and all of that. But don't worry, it won't be low key.'

In the event, they didn't go ahead, although they did holiday there, along with the children. But, as Pete himself remarked, it would have been unusual to renew their vows when they had only been married for less than a year.

That they genuinely cared about one another, whatever spats they might have had, was borne out by Kerrie-Ann Keogh, the Irish stylist who was regularly on hand to attend to them. Like many who worked closely with Katie and Pete, she saw a couple truly in love. 'I have worked with them at least every week for the past two years,' she said. 'They are a fabulous couple. They are the best and are so in love. Katie is fantastic to work with and is so much fun; she knows what she wants to wear and how she likes to look. Between them, I style music videos, calendars, press calls, fitness videos and red-carpet events. Kate loves pink and anything that sparkles. Pete is quite easy-going and likes his combats and T-shirts.'

Kerrie had also been charged with the responsibility of styling the wedding. 'I styled the bride and groom, bridesmaids, groomsmen, the dads, Harvey and the flower girls,' she said. 'It took around six months of preparation. My job was to make sure everything got done in time and was kept secret. I helped pull everything together. She just wanted to be like a princess and wanted the biggest dress possible. The wedding was a very enjoyable experience. But I didn't help Katie pick the dress.'

Meanwhile, the demands on the two grew. Everyone wanted a piece of them, and that included Mr Showbiz himself, Simon Cowell. There was a celebrity version of *The X Factor* coming up and he wanted the two of them on it: 'They're arguably the most famous couple in Britain,' he said. 'Everybody loves them and we'd love to have them sing for us. We are in advanced talks with them. We're always talking about contestants having *The X Factor* and, boy, do they have it.'

They certainly did. Every week they received an

increasing number of proposals, because every week they continued to make the headlines – no one could get enough of them. Their popularity seemed destined to soar and soar.

Another possibility was a joint album. Katie might have regretted her assault on Eurovision, but she had not put aside thoughts of making music her next career move, and, with Pete, she was in the perfect position to do so.

'Peter and Katie are deadly serious about making a proper chart assault as a pop duo,' said a source. 'Peter has been writing a lot recently and came up with material he wanted to perform with Katie. They want to release the album this year and go on tour before Christmas. Who knows, they might even have a go at landing the Christmas No. 1.'

As for a duet, they were rumoured to be thinking about the song 'Something Stupid', which again elicited a great deal of sniggering in the press – but why should they care? It was Katie and Pete, after all, who were laughing all the way to the bank.

But Katie didn't get everything she wanted: she let it be known that she'd be interested in a part in *Dr Who*, prompting scriptwriter and producer Russell T Davies, the man who had revived the programme's fortunes, to exclaim, 'Bless old Katie Price, but no way!'

Those setbacks were rare, however. The couple, and especially Katie, were moving towards national treasure status, unlikely as that might once have been. It was generally accepted that, with the two of them, what you see is what you get. They weren't pretending to be anything they weren't, and their popularity continued to swell as a result.

Nor was the interest confined to the UK. Katie went to the Far East on a promotional tour, only to find the people of China were even more flabbergasted by her figure than they were in Europe. 'Everybody out there was absolutely fascinated with my boobs,' she revealed. 'It doesn't seem like plastic surgery is that common over there, so they asked me about them in every single interview.'

Indeed, she seemed bemused that the Chinese, a nation famously good at finances, wanted to talk to her about her body rather than her business acumen, but, to the Chinese themselves, Katie must have seemed a very unusual person indeed.

Everything about the pair had now become a source of fascination, including their eating habits – and for girls who wanted to look like Katie, of course, *especially* her eating habits (which were not always that good). Katie revealed how she kept her tiny frame: 'If I'm feeling bloated in the morning, I'll have juice for breakfast, two litres of water during the day, then juice again in the evening. There have been remarks in the newspapers about how skinny I look, but, as a matter of fact, I have actually put on weight. I prefer being thinner – I hate my gut now,' she told one magazine.

Pete, however, was not so sure. 'I think she's too thin,' he said. 'I said to her, "Look, you don't need to be that thin, you gotta start eating now." She's getting better now and eating more. She did her fitness video and that's why she lost a lot of weight. She was rushing around everywhere too. She just needed to eat more junk!'

Katie's mother Amy agreed. She, too, was worried her daughter had been under a great deal of stress and wasn't eating properly, but she realised that Katie's appearance was crucial to her. It was, in part, what kept her in the public eye.

There was another slightly worrying note, as well, when Pete appeared to admit the two were not quite so close as they had once been, although he didn't say so in so many words. He was pleased, he admitted, that Katie covered up rather more than she used to, but was the intimate side of their relationship everything it had been?

'Now I know the woman comes home to me every day, I just wish she'd dress in her birthday suit for me more often,' he admitted. Nothing more came out at the time, but, given the later allegations that the marriage had been all but sexless as time went on, perhaps this was a harbinger of future problems. But, again, of course, no one realised it back then.

The two attracted plenty of people who wanted to emulate the couple's joint success, although ultimately no one was ever really able to, and among those trying to do so at this stage were Chantelle and Preston. Like Katie and Pete, they had met on a reality-television programme, in which Chantelle, who was not a celebrity, had had to convince everyone else that she was, and, also like Katie and Pete, the two were about to get married.

Chantelle also said that she wanted to emulate Katie, but the lady herself was none too pleased about it all. As far as Katie was concerned, she and Pete were the ultimate celebrity couple – and she didn't take kindly to anyone trying to steal their crown.

'Preston and Chantelle – I'm sick to death of reading that they're getting married,' she said. 'It's boring now. I liked her in the *Big Brother* house, but get a job now. Let's see if you can do something. There's no other couple like Pete and me. If anyone else is trying to be like us, they should stop now.'

Katie made the headlines again when she admitted to once experimenting with illicit substances, although a woman as driven, successful and in control as Katie would be unlikely to let anything go too far.

'I'm allergic to lots of things and it scares me to try anything,' she explained. 'It's just not me. I've only said I've done it once, as I like to be honest about things. If other people want to do it, it's up to them. If they're not strong enough to say no, then it's their problem. I'm a strong character, and I know what I do and don't want to do. Drink is enough for me. I never went to raves or anything like that.'

The rewards for how well they were doing were plain for all to see: in April 2006, Pete bought a £3.5 million holiday home in Cyprus. At the time, hopes were high for the future, but, ultimately, of course – and ironically – it was to act as his refuge when the marriage broke down. Right from the start, though, this did allow him to continue to connect to his Cypriot roots. Cyprus was where Pete hung out when his career took a nosedive – it meant a great deal to him and continued to act as a shelter whenever he needed it.

The problems that would ultimately bring down the relationship continued to appear. Being so in demand had its downside, not least in the toll it appeared to be taking on the couple's love life, as Pete had already hinted. Now it was Katie's turn to let slip that not all was well.

'I try, but we're both so busy and knackered,' she confessed. 'And obviously we've got two kids and they're a handful. I've been so busy this year. Because last year I was pregnant, so all the work we booked in, we had to do it this year.'

They did manage to be intimate occasionally, but even this seemed to bring problems in its wake. Both had often spoken of their desire to have another child, but early hopes that this was to come to fruition were dashed in July, when Katie suffered a miscarriage.

'It's impossible to describe how upset they both are,' said a friend. 'They wanted to keep the whole thing a secret and hoped no one would find out. She was only a few weeks into the pregnancy, but hadn't had her three-month scan, so had told only a handful of people.'

However, they did recover from this, and went on to try for more children.

Yet still there were ructions: Pete made the headlines by going public about his worries over Katie's drinking. 'I trust her when she's sober, but I don't trust her when she's drinking,' he admitted. 'It makes our relationship vulnerable. She really goes for it – she can't have just one or two.'

This was another foretaste of what was to come – Katie had been drinking the night the photograph that started everything off was taken – but, at the time, she merely lashed back in the public domain.

'I haven't got a drink problem, I'm not an alcoholic, I'm not a drunk,' she protested. 'I hardly ever drink. I'm a wife, I'm a mother. I'm not the girl I used to be when I was in my early twenties and single; I've changed so much. I used to go out to nightclubs and have a few drinks, but even then I didn't have a drink problem. I never have done. I used to get photographed on the occasional night out leaving a club, but I was a young, single girl and a lot of the time I was being paid to be there. Pete has issues with me drinking, just like other couples who don't like it when their partner changes after a drink.

'Pete doesn't like it when I've had a drink, but it's rare I get drunk. I've been drunk no more than four times this year and I will often go for weeks without a drop of alcohol. I have to get up with the kids at seven in the morning and I couldn't do that with a hangover. I don't even drink at home.'

Had they sorted the problem out back then, it might not have escalated in the way that it did – but they didn't. Of course, it all finally went wrong. But the differences of opinion about drinking, the rows and the lack of sex were all beginning to appear in mid-2006, when the couple hadn't even been married for a year. For a long time in the run-up to the separation, Pete was telling friends it was not 'if' they got divorced, but 'when' – and the problems can be traced back to then.

But in business matters there was further proof of Katie's acumen when she signed a deal with the Sheffield firm Panache for a new lingerie range. It looked to be a staggering success.

'The deal will be worth more than £5 million over the next few years. There has been a huge response from retailers,' stated Katie's manager, Claire Powell. 'Katie had a big say in the designs. They are all in very pretty pastel colours. Katie even has her own shade of pink and every item will have a bow, heart or both – they will become her trademarks. Every couple of months, different designs will be launched and the swimwear range will follow next year.'

But none of this was coming together by chance. Together, Katie and her manager had been planning ahead. 'We are both in this for the long term,' said Claire. 'And the current success is due to a well-thought-out business plan that we put together at the beginning of our relationship. While the Jordan brand may have a shorter shelf-life, Katie Price can go on and on. It's amazing how we can get Ann Summers ringing up for Jordan and Mothercare asking about Katie Price. Jordan's fan base is 90 per cent men, but Katie has a following which is 85 per cent women.'

The plan was working spectacularly well.

CHAPTER TEN
A WHOLE NEW WORLD

In the wake of the recent miscarriage, Katie and Pete's desire to have another child only deepened: the two were now said to be thinking of adoption as they looked to the future. They were also working on other projects as well. Towards the end of 2006, the couple were releasing an album of duets, *A Whole New World*, which led to Katie having another bout of worrying about her figure. This seemed to be even more of a preoccupation with her these days, once again leading observers to conclude she was feeling a degree of inner turmoil that was not obvious to the public. In truth, she had still not fully recovered from her post-natal depression and was more fragile than she appeared.

Not that you would have guessed it from listening to her: she was as upfront as she ever had been. Katie had decided to have a fourth operation on her breasts, but this time round it was to reduce them in size, and she was able to talk about it in her usual breezy manner. The glamour-model image was now a thing of the past, and Katie continued to shed all associations with what had gone before.

'I hate them. Get them out of me. Yuck!' she informed one startled interviewer. 'I'm having them reduced and I can't wait; I want them done by Christmas for Peter. They're saggy. Men may think they're great but they're just not pert any more and it's a turn-off. I used to love them but I don't need them any more. I hardly ever go out now; I'm always in with Peter, so I don't need to show them off. I want another baby, but I've got to get a boob job first.'

It was to work out the other way round, but no matter. Katie was as determined as ever on what she wanted to do next. Indeed, she made no secret of her predilection for plastic surgery and a boob job wasn't the only item on the cards. Katie again made it clear she had no intention of growing old as nature intended.

'When I'm older, I'm sure I'll have a nip/tuck here and there,' she said. 'I don't think it's a big deal. If I lived in America, no one would give a shit. Here it's like, "Oh, my God, surgery!" Maybe I should become an LA chick, then no one would say anything.'

In fact, she was to spend some time in LA with Pete, but found the town was not right for her.

Despite the odd bit of fractiousness, the couple were on the whole happy at this point. Home had become a haven away from the constant prying eyes of the camera, and they liked to relax and have people round. In this brief period of domesticity, glamour girl Jordan, who was always out on the tiles, had been comprehensively replaced by wife-and-mother Katie, who revelled in the comforts of family and friends, and who had no need to seek anything elsewhere. When asked how she chilled out, Katie replied, 'Just doing nothing. When people come to our house, they never want to leave because I have the heating on full blast, which drugs them. And we just watch DVDs and order takeaways. We've even had a park built for Harvey in the garden so we never have to go out – we're becoming recluses.'

They were certainly becoming rich; the new record was released at the same time Katie's D–G-cup lingerie range launched at Asda. The two of them hit the promotional tour, during which the full extent of the kind of life they were now living began to become clear. Pete might have been being tactful when he said the following, for he was in Scotland at the time, but, even so, it was obvious the couple were doing exceedingly well.

'Believe it or not, but I have a lot of property now,' he told one interviewer. 'I've started to manage property in Australia and Cyprus, and I'm wanting to start upping my portfolio in the UK. It's something I want to get really hands-on with next year. I've already started building an empire and I want to make it bigger and better, so I'd really like a place in Scotland.'

This was not his first time in Scotland, so he was able to talk about it with an informed eye. 'You know where I love in Scotland?' he asked. 'Glencoe. I've never seen anywhere so pretty. I visited back in 1998 with my brother Mike. We were coming down on a chairlift and it was so beautiful overlooking that valley with the snow; it was stunning. I'd buy a place up there, but I'd want it as a kind of getaway for me, Katie and the kids. It would be a great place to take the boys fishing when they're old enough.'

But Katie, a rather more hard-boiled individual than her husband, was not quite so tactful on the subject. 'I love coming up to Scotland, but it's always so cold,' she said. 'I'd have to have the log fire on all the time and I'd have to bring a bloody big jacket.'

In this period of happiness together, something else was on Pete's mind, too, and it was exactly the same thing that was preoccupying his wife. Property empires were one thing, but, to him, the good Mediterranean male, family was more important than anything else. And he wanted a bigger family of his own.

'I'd love it if Katie got pregnant this Christmas,' he confided. 'If she was to come over to me and say, "Here's your Christmas present, guess what?" that would just be unbelievable. But that's like wishing for a white Christmas.

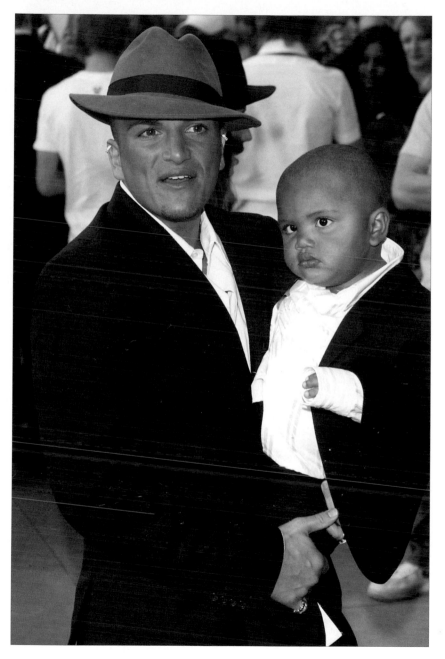

Peter quickly bonded with Katie's son, Harvey, from her prior relationship with footballer Dwight Yorke.

In early 2005, Katie became pregnant with her and Pete's first
child, Junior.

It wasn't long before Pete proposed.

Above: Katie shows off her engagement ring.   © *Getty Images*

Right: Katie and Peter release their first single together, *A Whole New World.*

Peter and Katie tied the knot on 10 September, 2005.

Above: Highclere Castle, the site of their fairytale wedding, with their enormous marquee on the grounds.

Below: The extravagantly beautiful wedding carriage, fit for any princess.

Above: Roadside congratulations for the happy couple en route to Highclere Castle.

Bottom left: Katie shows off her wedding ring and *right*, Pete's wedding ring.

Better together: Peter and Katie dominate the UK celeb scene and are frequently spotted out and about on the red carpet.

Katie is crowned 'Queen of the Mums' in 2007.

The happy family. Katie and Peter with their two sons Harvey and Junior.

If it comes, it comes. We are trying and I want a big family. My dad is one of twelve and I was one of six, so, if I follow tradition, by right, I should have three. That's the minimum amount. I'd love to have five.' It was a spookily accurate prediction. Counting Harvey, three is exactly the number of children he and Katie had, before they went their separate ways.

While all this was going on, however, Katie was also promoting her new lingerie range, and Pete had something to say about that, too. Namely, he wished he got the benefit of it. 'I bloody wish she'd come home and try the lingerie out on me,' he admitted. 'She comes home and takes them off – that's her work gear. That's why you shouldn't get married. Don't do it!' He was joking, of course, but jokes often contain a kernel of truth, and this one certainly did. He wasn't regretting marrying Katie, but the relationship was certainly showing some stresses and strains behind the scenes.

In fact, one aspect of her lingerie career was something of a sore point for Katie. She had not appreciated what had happened with Ultimo, and she was not afraid to say so. She was still on the promotional trail for her own brand of lingerie, and used the opportunity to make her views known. 'I would love to say that I was never, ever, ever the face of Ultimo,' she said passionately. 'All I did was one day for them for breast cancer.' Clearly, she was keen to emphasise her own brand was by far the better bet.

'My range is for women with bigger boobs and I've designed them personally,' she went on. 'People have been asking me to put my name to lingerie ranges for years, but I'm not that kind of person. If I'm going to do something, I want to be hands-on, I want to be involved with it. It's nearly two years ago I sat down and went through all my ideas with Asda and told them exactly what I wanted. They went away and came up with my ideas, and they were perfect. There is no other underwear range out there for people with busts over a D-cup that is really feminine, like my range.'

And then, of course, there was the album to promote, the proceeds of which were going to charity. Aware there was no shortage of critics when it came to her singing, Katie employed the time-honoured method of getting in there first. 'I'm the first person to slag off my voice,' she said. 'Do you know what? If people want to slag me off, I'll beat them to it. I was dreadful when I did Eurovision, absolutely diabolical, but that's brilliant because it made me think, If I ever want to have any sort of singing career, then I do have to have singing lessons, which is what I did. When people buy the album, they'll be eating humble pie because it's simply not the case any more. I definitely can sing and what I've done now makes me feel like a totally different person.'

It was certainly one of numerous examples that proved Katie would not allow herself to be knocked back. That was one of the reasons why she had become so wealthy, and now Pete was doing so, too. He was keen to make it plain, however, that the money he was getting was now off his own back and had nothing to do with his wife. Because Katie had been so much more high profile than her husband (and rather more successful), there had always been the cynics who cast aspersions on their differing earning powers, but Pete was having none of it.

'As soon as Kate accepted my marriage proposal, I made it clear I wanted to sign a pre-nup,' he revealed, in one of the many comments that was to have a poignant ring to it in light of the split. 'There was one reason and one reason only – so Kate would always know that I loved her for her and wasn't after any cash if things went wrong. At first, she was like, "Why do we need one? Do you think we're going to split up?" I said, "No, but now you'll never ever have it in your mind that I'm only with you for your money." I didn't want to give people any reason to ever say that to her.'

Pre-nups don't necessarily mean a great deal in the English legal system, but the point had been made: Pete was in this relationship for love, not money. Katie, meanwhile, wanted to make it clear that her husband had a career in his own right. 'I know people sometimes say things like, "I bet Pete ponces off her,"' she said. 'But he owns a nightclub and property in Cyprus and Australia and he has his own successful music career. Actually, you'd think he could take me shopping once in a while!'

And both were working hard. 'Since we got married last year, both our careers have done well,' added Pete. 'I may only do two or three things at once, compared to ten for Kate, but we've both been very successful... touch wood. We're both now financially secure but I'm glad we signed a pre-nup, just so she always knows how I feel.'

The relationship was still fundamentally solid, but something else was beginning to emerge. The couple were starting to argue far more publicly than they had ever done before, which was leading observers to wonder if, behind the scenes, something was beginning to go wrong. Katie was adamant this was not the case. 'Every time people see us on TV, even on something like *This Morning*, we bicker and argue,' she said. 'We're just so used to the cameras that we are completely ourselves; we're not putting on an act. You get other celebrity couples who don't seem real. You're always thinking, Is it going to last or isn't it? But we do normal, everyday things and people can relate to that. It's called being grounded and that's important to us.'

No doubt Katie felt that way, but the problem was that Pete didn't. All too often she appeared to be putting him down or drowning him out: essentially, hers was a combative personality, whereas the opposite applied to her husband. Pete, to a certain extent, wanted a quiet life – and Katie was not the person to give him that.

But what she had given him was a family life, and

clearly he relished that. He adored both the children, and loved the day-to-day routine of looking after them, as well. 'We're not trying to say we're miracle workers,' he said. 'We do have a nanny and people to look after the house, but we try to do as much as we can and we're not the type to go home and sit on the couch while someone else does the work. We like to get our hands dirty. Money can't buy normality – you have to do the simple things to achieve that.'

One of the less simple tasks that now lay ahead was stage performances, essential if the two of them wanted the album to sell. Chastened by her Eurovision performance, Katie was uncharacteristically nervous about what lay ahead. But there was an album to promote and the two of them had work to do, so she was being forced to face her fears and do what was needed next. And as someone not used to giving into her fears, and always open to exploring new opportunities, she did as she always did and got on with the job.

'It's all about confidence,' she said. 'Pete has been performing for years and his place is on stage, singing and dancing. With me, you could put me on stage modelling in my underwear in front of millions and I'd be fine, but ask me to sing and, because I'm not used to it, the nerves start.

'We have been doing a few gigs and lots of TV, though, so my nerves are getting much better now.'

She certainly wasn't displaying any nerves in November

2006, when she and Pete sang on the *Royal Variety Performance*. Before the show began, the couple were introduced to the Prince of Wales and the Duchess of Cornwall. Katie was looking radiant in another gown designed by Isabell Kristensen. This was another princessy style: a tight bodice and multi-layered tulle skirt, but it was Katie who complimented the Duchess, who was wearing Robinson Valentine, with characteristic self-confidence.

'Hello, nice to meet you, that's a lovely frock you've got there,' she said.

Indeed, it turned out that Charles and Camilla were fans. 'The Prince said, "Are you singing?" Katie told a reporter after the encounter. 'I told him we were, and he said, "Good." Camilla said, "I watched you together in the jungle." I'm not wearing this on stage,' Katie added of her frock. 'This is just for meeting them.'

And, in a strange way, it was a meeting of equals. On the one hand was real royalty; on the other, a couple at the peak of the showbusiness hierarchy. Indeed, most people could identify with Katie and Pete far more than they could with Charles and Camilla: this was the House of Windsor on a level playing field with the common man.

The dress Katie was wearing for the meeting made it look as if she was living in a fairytale and, a few weeks before Christmas, Pete's greatest wish came true. It was announced that Katie was pregnant again, with the baby due the following summer. Speculation had been mounting that she was pregnant, and, although she had been reluctant to confirm anything until matters were a little further advanced, Katie decided it was easier just to confirm what everyone already thought.

'I don't want to say too much because I'm not out of the woods and I don't want to jinx anything, but I'm due next summer,' said Katie tentatively. 'Because I had the miscarriage earlier this year, I'm really scared; that's why I'm saying earlier than I normally would. It's more stressful to keep it secret. I was relieved, but shocked because I've just got over the miscarriage. When we heard the heartbeat it was like, "Ahhh, that's good, it's there and everything is fine."'

And, indeed, all their fears were to be calmed in due course, when they had a happy, healthy baby. For now, at least, all was well in their world on many levels, although the arguing was never far away.

It was a joyful end to what had been a spectacular year, with Pete happily telling anyone who would listen that he'd been hoping for a baby for Christmas (rather more ominously, Katie observed that it must have been a fluke, given how busy they both were) and the couple ended the year with everything to look forward to. But problems were always in the offing, and, now, when they should have been looking forward to a happy event and a good year ahead, tragedy struck again.

A couple of days after Christmas, Harvey suffered burns

after an accident at home and had to be rushed to London's Chelsea and Westminster Hospital, where he was treated in the specialist burns unit. Initially, it was not clear what had happened. 'Harvey's in a stable condition, but that's all I know,' their manager Claire Powell told reporters. 'They are devastated, but they are being strong for Harvey.'

Meanwhile, their New Year's Eve party was cancelled and a trip to Australia put on hold.

A few days later, when Harvey was tentatively on the mend, the family released a statement to explain what had happened: it had been a freak accident that had taken place at home. 'It happened at the family home on Sunday afternoon when Harvey got in an empty bath with his clothes on and turned the hot tap, which scalded his right leg only,' it read. 'Harvey has been in hospital, with Peter and Katie by his bedside since the accident and, because of Harvey's medical condition, he needs to be monitored very closely.'

In the event, he was to spend just over two weeks in hospital and then needed further treatment as an outpatient, but fortunately went on to make a full recovery.

Because Katie was pregnant, she was not allowed to stay overnight at the hospital, in case she caught an infection which would harm the unborn child. Pete did the duties instead, but, for both, this was a gruelling period, with Katie spending as much time with her injured child as she was able to. 'I'd leave the hospital at 10.30pm and return by 7am,' she said. 'It was a very rough time. We were knackered and worried sick about Harvey. Because he is partially sighted, he would shout "Daddy" to make sure Pete was with him in the room before he could sleep.'

Unsurprisingly, she voiced a wish that Dwight would take on some of Harvey's care, but it didn't look very likely. 'It would be a relief for us if Dwight ever offered to have Harvey for a night, never mind a weekend,' she admitted. 'Harvey needs four lots of medicine in the morning, three in the afternoon and another four at night, which includes an injection which Pete or I give him. He is hard work. I'm not complaining, just explaining. I couldn't cope with Harvey without Pete and my mum Amy.'

The whole household loved Harvey, but the younger members of it were learning to treat him with care. 'Junior adores Harvey, he copies him,' said Katie. 'But he's already learned that, if he winds him up, Harvey will get frustrated and whack him. Junior is a mini Pete – he loves to show off to the camera. I love them both to bits, even though I still feel guilty about the early days after I gave birth to Junior and couldn't bond with him because of depression.'

Bonding had subsequently taken place, of course, but the depression was still there and might well have contributed to the problems that were slowly building in the relationship. At least the latest pregnancy was progressing well. According to Pete, Katie had developed cravings for peas and Lucozade, and in every other respect was healthy, as was the unborn child. But other problems remained, as well. Despite it now being eighteen months since the birth of Junior, and the fact that she was now pregnant with her third child, the depression had not entirely lifted, and it was taking its toll.

'I want to know when it will be over,' admitted Katie on ITV's *This Morning*. 'I'm still taking medication.' She related how she'd been feeling jealous and paranoid of her nanny, adding, 'I thought my kids didn't want me.'

It was yet another worrying sign that, although the couple's world might have looked gilded from the outside, inside there was quite another tale to tell.

It was because of this rather more serious aspect of her life that Katie was now introduced to another member of the Royal Family – the Queen. The occasion was the opening of a children's centre at the Moorfields Eye Hospital, where Harvey had been a long-term patient, and so Katie was an obvious person to be present. With her high profile and the fact that it was common knowledge that she had a disabled child, again, she was able to speak volumes for parents in the same position simply by being there. Pete and Harvey were also in attendance, and Harvey himself greeted the monarch with the phrase, 'Hello, your Majesty.'

The Queen, who, if she was nonplussed to be meeting Katie, certainly didn't show it, asked how Harvey was getting on. 'He has been here from day one,' Katie told her. 'He can see shapes and colours now. He's really improving and he's four and a half now.'

Afterwards, Katie was impressed. 'She was actually quite chatty,' she told waiting reporters. 'I thought, We're having a conversation here. She was really concerned and asked how long he had been here. She said he's in the right place.'

Pete was equally forthcoming. 'He's been through a lot,' he said. 'We're no different from any other family. You can really see how he's improved. It was a real honour to meet the Queen.'

But it was this more serious side to their life that was actually making the couple so many fans. Katie's resilience in the face of her son's illness and Pete's obvious bond with the boy he treated as his own were just two of the reasons why the public couldn't get enough of them. In March 2007, Katie was named Grattan Celebrity Mum of the Year, another clear sign that the public now saw her as Katie, not Jordan.

The head of Grattan, Mike Hancox, saw that side of her, too. 'The general public showed in their voting just how much they respect and admire her as a mother,' he said. 'Katie has become a symbol of how a person can be constantly in the public eye, whilst remaining a devoted and doting mum.'

The competition had certainly been stiff. Other

contenders included Katie's great rival Victoria Beckham, the Duchess of York, Davina McCall, Kate Moss and the late Jade Goody, then just out of the racism row on *Big Brother*. As for Katie herself, it was a vindication of who she was and all she had done. 'Years ago I used to get called the mother from hell because I was younger going out and now it's all turned round – what makes a good mum, you tell me, I don't know,' she said. 'What I think is a good mum is probably different from what other people think is a good mum. There is no role model for me. I am what I am, and to be honest it was really good meeting the Queen, but at the end of the day it's just the Queen. To me, everyone should be equal... If you say the word "mummy", he [Harvey] says, "Beautiful," and, if you say, "Daddy," he says, "Daddy's good-looking."'

Good mum as she was, Katie was certainly looking forward to the birth of her next child. She still hadn't had that breast reduction, and was looking forward to it more and more. The effects of the pregnancy, of course, had made what was already in situ even bigger, but she couldn't have the necessary operation until the baby arrived.

'They have got huge,' she confessed. 'I am one million per cent having a boob job after the birth. It will be my fourth, but I want new implants, possibly smaller, and to perk them up a bit. And if I have a new boob job they will be exclusive to Pete – nobody else will have touched them. Pete is fascinated by my huge boobs. He calls them my "gazallas" and asks if he can touch them, but sometimes they are so sore I snap his head off. He likes to bury his head in them and for me to squash them together so he almost suffocates.'

Happy as her new size made Pete, however, Katie was not at all comfortable with her body in its heavily pregnant state. It wasn't just the size of her breasts that was bugging her, it seemed everything else was as well. 'I'm not enjoying this pregnancy,' she said. 'I'm the biggest I've ever been; I can't bear to look at myself in the mirror. I can still get my legs and bum into my size-zero jeans but I'll be doing my DVD workout and juicing regime to get back in shape after the birth. I'm also going to have Botox, the works. It's what I'm looking forward to the most.'

However, according to Katie, she and Pete still had a very fulfilling personal life. 'My sex life is brilliant this time round,' she said. 'Even though I'm suffering terrible back pain, Pete and I have been inventive. Pete is really fit and toned, and looks incredibly sexy. We have sex in all different ways to get round my backache.'

But it was a very different story from the last time around. 'When I was pregnant with Junior, my sex life was non-existent because I was depressed,' she admitted. 'I still take anti-depressants, but am weaning myself off them and will be clear by the time our baby is born. I'm scared that the depression will come back, but this time I'm going to do everything differently. I'm taking eight weeks off work – the longest in my life – and, because I'm a naturally stressy person, I've learned relaxation techniques. Now I just want to get the birth over with. The worst thing is that I can't ride my horse because of my back. I rode right up to the last minute with Junior and Harvey.'

As interest in the couple was as strong as ever, they had signed up for their next reality-television show, *Katie & Peter: The Next Chapter*. There was also some interest shown in them from the States. Katie was thrilled by this, and used it as an opportunity to make a dig at her old rival Victoria Beckham. 'We're really excited,' she said. 'The only other British couple beginning to make it in America are the Beckhams. I hear Victoria and David are making a one-hour show. We'll be on eight times a week, with a three-hour show each Saturday. At the end of the day, she's just a footballer's wife and Pete and I are still individuals in our own right.'

In truth, of course, not only did Victoria have a work schedule and a work ethic to rival Katie's but she and David had already cracked America, a notoriously difficult gig for any British star.

Beauty treatments after the birth of the baby were not the only thing on Katie's mind. She had turned novelist, was working on a series of children's books based on ponies and was also planning her latest lingerie launch, as the last had been a stunning success.

'I'm a workaholic and I love what I do,' said Katie. 'Pete

and I have never been happier. We do find time to relax –
we're both taking helicopter lessons. We want one so we
can avoid traffic. The only time we really argue is in the car.
I think I'm a much better driver, and vice versa, so it will be
interesting to see what happens in the helicopter!'

The trouble was that this was not the only time they
really argued. Katie was a highly competitive woman and it
was beginning to show in relation to the one man she really
didn't have to compete with – Pete. But it wasn't in her
nature to take a back seat to anyone, or even to share the
drive, and very soon the strain would start to show. Pete
was to admit that there had been problems in the
relationship for at least two years before the final split: it
was now the spring of 2007. Very soon, the foundations of
those rows would be laid and would finally tear them apart.

CHAPTER ELEVEN

CONQUERING AMERICA

A ll British entertainers, whether they admit it or not, have one wish in common: to conquer the United States. Success in the UK is seen as small beer compared to making it big in the land of opportunity across the pond, and Katie and Pete felt that as much as anyone else. There had also been much talk to the effect that Katie was just the sort of person to make it in the States.

Hardworking and ambitious, her appearance was also similar to some of America's biggest idols – most notably Pamela Anderson and, to a lesser extent, the late Anna Nicole Smith. In truth, Katie would never have become another Anna Nicole. Far more in control of herself and her destiny, she would never, even in her darkest moments, allow her life to run as out of control as Anna Nicole to tragic effect did hers, but they were both outrageous pneumatic blondes (and, in Katie's case, also brunette) with the common touch. And since Anna's death there was, to put it bluntly, a gap in the showbiz roster to fill.

And then there was Pete. America is a notoriously tough nut for a British – or, in this case, Australian – singer to crack, but that didn't mean it couldn't be done. So often the rather overlooked part of the partnership, Pete had, after all, made a name for himself in his own right and, with all the publicity the two of them managed to generate together, there seemed no reason why he couldn't give it a shot.

They timed their launch in with the third series of their reality-TV show *Katie & Peter: The Next Chapter*, which was about to air; it was to be the usual fly-on-the-wall documentary about the couple's life with their family. However, not only was it to be shown on ITV2, where it became the station's most-watched programme, it was also to air in the States. What the American audience made of it would be some kind of indicator as to their chances of success over there and hopes were high that it would make quite a splash. The American appetite for reality TV was quite as strong as the British one, although, if truth be told, they probably hadn't seen anything quite like this before.

Filming had started around Christmas, at about the time of Harvey's accident, and so that was featured, along with the couple's increasing series of arguments. Was it staged for the cameras, or was the arguing for real? The ructions certainly made for good viewing, but it was becoming increasingly and uncomfortably obvious that the rows were indeed real. They were to develop a nasty edge too, as with the row that aired just before the final break. But, at the time, everyone played it down.

'Before school, it's crazy in the morning, like any household,' Katie told an interviewer. 'You'll see it all in our new show – food shopping, nappy buying, shopping for a new car and plenty of bickering, of course! The kids have their baths around 6.15pm. I love that time of the evening. Pete and I bath them and put them to bed. I treasure those special family moments so much.'

But that mention of bickering was very telling. It was increasingly a part of their lives, but Katie clearly didn't realise that Pete was nothing like as light-hearted about it as she was. Had the couple been able to sort out their growing problems back then, perhaps the split might have been averted.

Pete, however, was putting a good face on it for now. 'We argue about everything,' he admitted. 'We're complete opposites, but for some reason we attract. I never believed that opposites attract until I met Kate. It works. I don't know how, and yet it does.'

What was subsequently to prove the case, of course, was that it worked while the two were still in the first flush of attraction. When that began to fade, the arguing took on a very different complexion indeed. But, for now, all was outwardly calm. The duo and their offspring set off to launch a charm offensive on LA. The first job was to find a house. 'The kids need their routine and stability. Spending long periods of time in LA will only be possible when we have a base,' Katie told an interviewer just before they set off. 'We'll find a nursery for the children so they can have friends to play with while we're out there. I can't stand staying in hotels.'

Pete, who would eventually take to LA far more than his wife, was equally enthusiastic. 'I want to be able to teach Junior to swim,' he said. 'Harvey can already swim. He was going twice a week before his accident on New Year's Eve. Junior has lessons every Saturday. I also want a house with a gym because I'm really into working out again. I've been going four or five times a week and I'm watching what I eat. If I keep going like this, I'll be in really good shape for the summer.'

Of course, there was already a famous English couple over there – the Beckhams. But mention of this to Katie was like a red rag to a bull. 'Victoria's gone to LA because of David's transfer to LA Galaxy,' she said. 'She's gone over there as his wife, not because of her work. I don't intend meeting up with her out there. We have our own friends there, like Simon Cowell. We're looking forward to having dinner with him. I'm over Posh and Becks.'

You could say that again. When Pete ventured he might

like to see Becks in action, Katie lost no time in knocking that idea on its head. 'We didn't go to the Oscars this year because we didn't want to turn up with our friends on the red carpet and create a hype,' said Pete. 'That might work for the Beckhams but it's not the way that Katie and I are, we don't need to name-drop. I might go and watch David play, though – I'd like that.'

'No way, Pete! We'll be far too busy,' snapped Katie. 'And, besides, why would you want to watch football? You can see that on TV over here. I'd rather throw myself into the American culture and watch basketball or baseball.'

The lady had spoken and that was that.

Katie clearly couldn't bear to let this one rest. Her first big interview in the States took place on the entertainment programme *Extras*, on which the two of them appeared to promote their new reality show. Katie was asked about Posh and Becks.

'Who?' was her response.

'I might as well say it, she is better-looking than Victoria, but I'm not as good-looking as David,' said Peter, appearing to pour oil on troubled waters.

But Katie wasn't having any of that either. 'It's not hard to be better-looking than her, is it really?' she asked. 'She's just a footballer's wife and Pete and I are still individuals.'

Another problem that was beginning to surface was in the bedroom. In the early months of her pregnancy, Katie had talked about how her hormones made their relationship even more passionate, but this was clearly not the case any more.

'I feel really big, my back hurts and I'm knackered, so the last thing I want to do is have sex – I feel really gross all the time,' said Katie, as she revealed that she got Pete to put on an empathy bag. 'Now he can appreciate what I'm going through. I thought it would be funny to put Pete in one for a few hours – he immediately started complaining about backache, his breathing... everything.'

Pete took it in very good part, but, according to some reports after they split, their sex life never really recovered from that period in their lives.

There was another setback with the launch of their reality show in the States: it didn't receive anything like the rapturous reception everyone was hoping for. Their dreams of conquering America, although not totally dashed for some time yet, certainly seemed a long way from reality, given the tenor of some of the reviews. Americans didn't get Katie one bit and her particular brand of Britishness left them totally cold.

'It is the most irrelevant reality show – for Americans, at any rate – in the history of irrelevant reality shows,' wrote the critic Linda Stasi. 'This mess, called *Katie & Peter*, stars a couple of low-rent British celebrities. One is Katie Price, aka Jordan, a glamour model, which means that she's famous for her giant double-F implants, which she once removed and sold on eBay, and also for her constant need to pose naked.

'The boyfriend of Katie/Jordan is someone called Peter Andre, a creepy crooner in the order of a modern-day Tom Jones – without cleverness.'

And so it went on. Other reviewers were only too happy to lay it on with a trowel, too. For once, the biter was bitten. Katie certainly knew how to dish it out, but now she had to stand back and take it, too.

Reaction, it must be said, was totally different back in the UK, not least because the couple were so popular. Katie's braveness, when it came to Harvey, was undisputed, as was her ability simply to get on with life. Pete, meanwhile, was an engaging man with a charming personality, and the two could simply do no wrong. The reviews were much kinder: the real sticking point seemed to be that the States just didn't get *Katie & Peter*. They were a particularly British phenomenon, sometimes reminiscent of nothing so much as a naughty seaside postcard, and amid all the nonsense was a certain amount of self-deprecation that the Americans simply couldn't understand. Not that Katie and Pete were concerned: neither appeared unduly worried by their lack of popularity Stateside and, as ever, got on with the job in hand.

Their lives continued to be wracked with drama, though. Back in the UK, as so often, near tragedy struck when it was least expected. Just a couple months on from Harvey's dreadful accident, it was Pete's turn to be laid low, having been admitted to the East Surrey Hospital in

Redhill, suffering from suspected meningitis. As ever, it was their spokeswoman who handled the news. 'Following recent tests on Peter Andre at the East Surrey Hospital, it is believed that Peter is suffering from suspected meningitis,' the statement read, going on to ask that, '...for Katie to continue as normal, and support Peter and the family at this worrying time, we would ask all the press to respect Peter and Katie's privacy, and to not contact or visit the hospital.'

The news couldn't have come at a worse time. Katie was by now heavily pregnant, still suffering the effects of the depression and still looking after her numerous business projects, while the couple had such a demanding schedule that it was hard for them to take any time off at all. But this time they had to for Pete was plainly very ill.

'When he was taken to hospital, he was so weak he had to be helped on board the ambulance,' said a friend. 'Katie is frantic with worry. Obviously she's desperate to get to the bottom of what's wrong.'

There was also a fear that Katie might develop the illness herself – no joke when she was just two months away from giving birth – and so she was torn between spending as much time with Pete as she could, and keeping a sensible distance so that she wouldn't do anything to harm the unborn child. A further fear about Katie contracting the disease herself was that it might send her into early labour and, after all the problems with

Harvey, the last thing the couple wanted was anything that might harm their newborn.

Pete's mother Thea flew in from Cyprus to add her support, both to her son and her exhausted daughter-in-law, while his brother Chris, resident in Australia, sounded a slightly cheerier note when he said, 'Peter sounded groggy on the phone, but he'll be OK. We're a tough bunch.'

Katie herself, though, seemed shell-shocked by it all. Encountering a group of photographers waiting outside the hospital, she merely said, 'I don't want to talk, it's too distressing. I just want to see Peter.'

But at least the doctors were by now fairly sure that it was viral meningitis – nasty, but not as bad as bacterial meningitis. But it was an immensely worrying time.

In the event, Pete was allowed home after about two weeks, frail but on the mend. 'He now needs to be left alone with his family to recover and we ask that all the press respect Peter and Katie's privacy at this time,' said their spokeswoman.

Pete himself said that he was 'over the moon' to be going home; he had been on a drip but was now pronounced well enough to be taken off it. He was so weak that he'd been forced to use a wheelchair, but, in a determined show of strength, managed to leave the hospital on his own two legs and get to the car. It had been a nasty experience, one that the couple were happy to put behind them.

Katie had, in fact, been thoroughly shaken by what had happened. For once, that famous resilience appeared to falter: the thought that she might actually have lost her husband was a hard one to bear, but she put a brave face on it. 'Pete was never going to die, although he was worried that he might,' she said in an interview at the time. 'I knew he wouldn't leave me. I wouldn't say that it's changed me, although it's brought us even closer together, if that's possible. Me and the kids missed him so much when he was in hospital – the kids were so sad without him around to play with. I went to the hospital as much as I could to be with him. I took pictures of the kids in for him to look at and things like my pyjamas, too, so it smelled like home.'

It would have been an ordeal whenever it happened, but of course the pregnancy made it all the worse.

'Suddenly I found myself heavily pregnant and Pete wasn't there to support me,' said Katie. 'I had some tough days trying to get to the hospital, do the shopping, deal with the kids and the animals; sometimes it just got to be too much. But he's on the mend now. Pete's not better, he's still frail and weak, but he's recovering. All of us have been in hospital for one reason or another this year. It's been tough, one drama after another. I usually rise to an emotional challenge, but it's been harder this time because I'm so heavily pregnant. I'm tired constantly and more emotional – and my back gets really bad when I'm pregnant. I was never going to crack, I'm a strong woman, but I'm glad the worst is behind us. Now we can look forward to our new baby.'

In hindsight, this should have been the time when the family clung together more closely than ever. Having had a run of accidents and illnesses, everyone involved, especially the adults, knew what they would lose. At least all the recent traumas highlighted what was important in life, and Katie knew it, too.

'We're going to take some time to enjoy being a family,' she said. 'We're stronger than ever. Nothing and no one can come between us. I am more excited about our future than ever. Sure, I've had tough times with Pete and Harvey, but unfortunately that's life. It just goes to prove that you should live each day as if it's your last.'

She was absolutely right, but that didn't stop the rumour mill. Behind the scenes, speculation was growing that all was not well. In the past, the couple were forced to endure plenty of whispering about their relationship, mainly to the effect that it was a publicity stunt. Eighteen months down the line, with one child and another on the way, at least no one was saying that any more. But someone, somewhere, had by now got the impression that something was amiss.

Katie ignored it all, talking brightly about going back on her juice diet after the baby was born, and full of plans for the future. 'Hopefully, my body will ping back into shape,' she said. 'I'll follow a harsh exercise regime, too – an aerobic fat-burner or full-body workout every day. I don't have any stretch marks, but I don't intend to ever let my shape slip just because I've had kids. I'm determined to get back into my bikini after the baby. I'll be back in it in three weeks, sitting around my pool, enjoying the summer sunshine with my kids. But I don't want to put too much pressure on myself this time as I have a busy autumn and winter, and need to be healthy to cope with all that.'

Indeed she did. Katie still had projects coming out of her ears, and the one that seemed closest to her heart involved horses, books and children. She had, after all, been obsessed with horses all her life and her enthusiasm was palpable when she talked.

'The pony novels are based on my experience when I was younger,' she said. 'I love horses, but I always had the ugliest pony because my mum couldn't afford much and there was always someone at the stable yard who had a better horse and better equipment. I had horse posters on my bedroom wall, never boy bands. I love horses, so I'm so pleased to be doing these children's books.'

Indeed, her love of horses was highlighted again when she was spotted at Royal Ascot, another indication that she was beginning to change the circles in which she moved. After all, Katie had met both the Queen and Prince Charles by now, even if it was in a working environment, and there were growing signs that she was starting to get involved in the horsey county set. But this was not something she could share with Pete and ultimately it was yet another thing that would tear them apart.

She was certainly happy planning for the future: one minute revealing that she wanted to have six children, the next that the new arrival was going to be a girl. 'I'm very excited. I've got my three boys and a little princess,' she said.

Apparently, Pete took note of that remark, for he was the one who was to come up with the unusual name for their youngest child.

That child arrived shortly afterwards, on 29 June 2007. Katie was ensconced in London's Portland Hospital where the little girl, 6lb 13oz, emerged via a Caesarian. As with Junior, an ecstatic Pete appeared shortly afterwards to talk about the new arrival. 'I am a very happy man now; my beautiful wife gave birth to a beautiful baby girl,' he said. 'She's absolutely stunning, beautiful. I am really, really happy.'

His daughter's name was to be a very unusual one, but the couple hadn't come up with it yet. Asked what the name would be, Pete replied, 'We haven't chosen one yet. I mentioned Crystal, but we are not going to end up calling her that. At the moment we are just going to call her baby.'

Crystal was the title of one of Katie's books, and Katie herself had already pronounced on the matter: 'I won't be calling her a silly name, like Apple, Peaches or Carrot,' she said.

Pete looked to be becoming a typically protective Mediterranean father as well. 'She's not going out until she is 64,' he declared. 'Maybe when she's thirty, she can go out with her girlfriends, but that's about it.' He was overprotective 'with the boys', he admitted, adding, 'I don't want to think about other children, at least not for a while.'

It was, of course, hardly surprising he was over-protective given Harvey's problems and how much scrutiny both children were under. The pressure would only increase now the youngest child had arrived.

Pete was revelling in it, though, as any proud father would. Asked who the baby took after, he said, 'At the moment I can't tell. I probably will be able to in another few days. I suppose she looks like a bit of both. I just hope she ends up looking just like Katie. It will be nice for her – Junior looks like me.'

Amid all the happiness, though, was another ominous hint of what was to come. Pete adored being a father again, but was again finding the bedroom a problematic area. 'I think she's got post-husband depression – she's not giving me any love at all,' he admitted.

He was making light of it but, again, there was more than a hint that all was not well. Of course, most women don't feel like resuming their love lives immediately after giving birth, but in this case they were never to return to the early days of passion. All sorts of problems were beginning to appear that would simply grow over the next few years.

It took a few weeks before they decided on a name but, when they did, it was unusual, to say the least. The little girl was to be called Princess Tiáamii. This was because she was a princess to them, her parents explained, while the second part of the name was with reference to their two mothers, Thea and Amy, with an accent and a few 'i's added on to make it stand out. It certainly did that. The name was Pete's idea and one that he was given a good deal of praise for – in the world of celebrity, parents like their children to stand out from the crowd, and this name certainly made the newborn do that.

But was their family life now back on course? The signals were increasingly mixed. The biggest hint to date that not everything in the garden was rosy came shortly after the name was chosen, and it appeared, briefly, to date back to the life Katie had had before she met Pete – clearly not a good sign. Katie was seen drinking at a nightclub, an image more readily associated with the Jordan days than the life she had now. Worse still, quite suddenly, she seemed to be getting very bored with that life.

'I'm never in the papers any more,' she was heard to say. 'It's 'cos I'm a mum and I'm boring and I stay in.' And as for Peter – 'We're always arguing – just like on our TV programme,' she continued. 'When the cameras stop, we still argue. He gets a lot of attention and we're both really jealous.'

To make matters worse, she was reported to have been sick in the loos on her night out.

This was not the Katie people were getting used to, and, while she might not have been in the papers as much as she had been in the earlier days, she was more successful than ever. Everything she touched turned to gold. And indeed, shortly after that, matters were back to normal, in public at least, as she talked about her life. She was launching a new perfume, Stunning, and was as eager to share as she had ever been. And, if truth be told, the public wanted the family to be all right. The British love nothing more than a fairytale and tend to be heartbroken if it turns sour, as in the case of Charles and Diana. They simply didn't want Katie and Pete to split.

Certainly, the new addition to the family was bringing nothing but joy. Katie was loving having a daughter at last and couldn't wait to start dressing her in her mother's favourite colour. 'It's fantastic,' she said. 'Having a girl is brilliant because I finally have a child I can dress up in pink clothes! When she's older, I'm hoping she'll give me support so we can gang up against the boys. With a daughter, our family feels complete... I want another five kids, so that's eight in all. Then I want to adopt more. Pete's all for it, and it'll be a great excuse to buy a bigger house.'

She was, however, going to take a short break. 'It'll be a

few years before I have another child,' she admitted. 'Since *I'm A Celebrity...* it seems like I've spent the last three years pregnant. My body is in desperate need of a rest and I'd like to concentrate on my career before number four.'

For all her remarks about boredom, domesticity clearly still held a strong appeal. When the relationship worked between them, Katie was happy to stay at home and look after her family, as well as building up her external career. There was another highly ominous note, though, when she was asked if there was any competition between herself and her husband. 'Not at all,' was her reply. 'People often think, What does Pete actually do?, but he's been doing very well investing in property abroad and he has a studio at home, where he's writing music for other people. He's also making a new album of his own at the moment. But we don't have to justify ourselves to people: we have nothing to prove to anyone. We've been filming our show since January, until the baby was born, so it's nice to have a rest now.'

The trouble was, though, that, while Pete did indeed have plenty of projects on the go, he was carrying nothing like the workload of his fiercely ambitious wife. It simply wasn't in his nature. He was as laidback as she was fiery, content to go with where life took him as she was determined to carve out the path that she alone chose. All the hints that something was going wrong were there: both admitted on various occasions that their sex life was suffering, their arguments had become more frequent, on- and off-screen, and, most damaging of all, there was no way round the fact that Katie was a lot more successful than Pete. It shouldn't have mattered, but it did. They might have had a far greater impact together than they ever could apart, but it was still Katie who was the driving, domineering force behind it all. It was increasingly obvious by now that this was going to end in tears.

The nightclub incident might have been a one-off, but there were clear signs that Katie wanted to be getting out there and taking on the world in order to show what she could do. 'I'm more ambitious than ever,' she declared. 'Having kids motivates me because I want them to have the lifestyle that I have when they're older. I like being knocked down by people who criticise me – it makes me more determined to do better.'

It was an attitude that would take her far, but it was also a sign that she was a very tough woman, prepared to take on anyone – and Pete was simply not in the same mould.

The latest project, of course, was her scent. Katie, clever businesswoman that she was, was not going to lose control of any part of the process and, naturally, she was keeping an eye on the whole project from start to finish. 'I smelled Britney Spears' and J-Lo's and I quite liked them,' she said of the competition. 'I haven't smelled Jade's [Goody] and I wouldn't want to. I'm not interested in buying anything of hers after the way she behaved on *Celebrity Big Brother*.

I've been involved with it all, right from the start. I drew bottle designs, chose the picture, the packaging and, most importantly, I chose the fragrance itself. It's been a long process. [It smells] sweet and soft, with hints of jasmine and mandarin: strong, but floral. I chose it because I'd wear it, but I want women of all ages to like it.'

As for Pete – 'He loves it. In fact, when I wear it, he can't keep his hands off me! I'm sure, when women wear it, it will turn their men on. It's a great pulling perfume.'

This was slightly at odds with the interviews both she and Pete gave about their love life – or lack of it – these days, but, still, no matter. With Princess Tiáamii newly on the scene, the two were desperate to make the relationship work, but, away from the spotlight, it was becoming increasingly difficult to do so. Katie's focus on her career was also absolute. 'I want to push my brand worldwide,' she said. 'I'm planning a range of other products for the body, like soaps and shower gel. I've also got plans for a range of bed linen and make-up. My attitude to business is that I don't want something to happen, because I know it's going to happen; I'll never stop. Pete and I are going to the US in the winter as our reality-TV show, *Katie & Peter*, has done really well there. I have my autumn/winter lingerie coming soon. I also want to do a film about my life.'

It was certainly quite the time for celebrity scents: Katie's Stunning got to the number-one slot at retailer Superdrug on the week of its release, only for it to be knocked into second place the following week, when Kate Moss launched a perfume entitled Kate. Other strong contenders came from Victoria Beckham (natch) and Gwen Stefani. But the message was clear: brand Katie was bigger than ever – and it was growing still.

CHAPTER TWELVE
KATIE PRICE, INC.

By summer 2008, everything was going so well career-wise that Katie applied to register her name, Katie Price, as a trademark. All in all, she had sold a combined total of over three million copies of her books and, better still, her novel *Crystal* was revealed to have outsold the entire six titles that made up the shortlist for the Man Booker prize. Meanwhile, she and Pete were starting their latest television venture: a chat show called *Katie & Peter: Unleashed*. It was as popular as anything they'd done but it was clear that here was no Michael Parkinson in the making. Katie, meanwhile, had been voted Woman of the Year by *Cosmopolitan* magazine – her popularity was soaring to ever-greater heights.

As ever, though, drama was never far away. This time it came courtesy of *Heat* magazine in a move that astounded even other media outlets. They published a sticker with a picture of Harvey and the words 'Harvey wants to eat me'. Katie and Pete complained to the Press Complaints Commission, as did 56 of the magazine's readers: it was a joke that had been allowed to get out of hand. The magazine gave away fifty stickers in that particular issue, including one of a picture of Britney Spears and the words 'Mum of the Year', and another of Victoria Beckham posing beside the legend 'Will you fucking smile?'

The Harvey sticker, like the others, was clearly intended as some sort of post-modern irony, but the widespread viewpoint was that it was not that amusing to make fun of a disabled child. Katie and Pete were incandescent and this time there wasn't a soul who didn't agree with their point of view. Certainly, *Heat*'s actions seemed utterly inexplicable to them and everyone else.

'I want to know what exactly they meant by this,' said Katie in a furious outburst. 'I want to know how they sat around in their editorial meeting and justified making fun of a five-year-old child who can't even talk. If it's to have a go at me, they can do that without being cruel to my son. People can take the mickey all they like out of me and my husband – we're grown-ups and we can answer back, but we're talking here not just about a little boy, but a little boy who's disabled.'

She had an exceptionally good point. Their actions came across as bullying of the worst sort. 'What they've done here is not only cruel, it shows they're totally ignorant about Harvey's condition,' Katie continued. 'They are making out that Harvey is fat because he is greedy and eats all the time. In fact, his size is down to his thyroid not working properly; he needs special medication every day just to keep him going. So, if they attack my son because of his size, which is a result of his disability, they're actually attacking him because he's disabled. What are they going to mock him for next – the colour of his skin? What they're saying is that it's fine to take the piss out of a disabled child. Well, I'm saying it's not. This is a form of bullying and I hate bullying of any kind. Like every other parent of a disabled kid, I've worked long and hard to get people to treat my son in a normal way.'

A lot of media commentators, in normal circumstances not necessarily Katie's biggest fans, rallied to the cause, with quite a few calling this a new low in British journalism. In the event, *Heat* grovelled, publishing an apology on its website. Under the heading 'Harvey – Sorry', it said, 'We now accept the decision to include this sticker was a mistake and we recognise it has caused offence, not only to Katie and Peter Andre, but to a number of readers. Immediately following publication, we apologised unreservedly to Katie and Peter. We wish to apologise publicly to Harvey, Katie and Peter for any embarrassment and distress caused.'

It had been an ugly episode and one which has not really been explained to this day.

The New Year began on a cheerier note. Katie and Pete were filming their reality show, *The Next Chapter*, in the course of which they visited the jungle where they had met and fallen in love just four years earlier. At long last, she had had the breast reduction she'd been talking about, too, although she was uncharacteristically keeping covered up. Katie also spoke out against animal cruelty, realising that, with her profile, it was possible to use it to do some good.

There had been signs that Katie was getting restless, although nothing had become too public as of yet. But the full extent of recent problems, including Katie's depression and extended periods of no sex, were coming to light. Even the wedding had been fraught. 'I was a psycho the first time we got married,' Katie told Paul O'Grady, as she discussed plans for the two of them to renew their vows. 'I had such bad post-natal depression.' On another occasion, she commented, 'When I had Junior and I had post-natal depression, we obviously argued a lot. Then, after Princess, there was another little moment because I was tired and Pete's dad was ill, and there was stress about that – but now we're back to normal.'

It was clear that there had been real problems behind the scenes, but Katie saw the renewal of the wedding vows as the start of a whole new phase in their lives. 'I'll be changing my name to Katie Andre when I get round to it too,' she revealed. 'The only reason I haven't is because it takes ages. I'll stay Katie Price professionally, but it would be nice to be Katie Andre in my cheque book and passport.'

Another milestone was coming up, too: Katie's thirtieth birthday. It's an occasion that makes many women sit up and take note, while Katie herself had already fitted in as much in her life to date as a whole army of women. There was talk of the Katie Price empire expanding: her pony books were winning awards and it seemed the country, quite simply, loved her. At any rate, she was determined to do something special for the big day.

'It won't be like the wedding, but it'll be huge,' Katie told an interviewer. 'It's got a theme but I can't tell you what it is. Only I can get away with it, put it that way – very over the top. Everyone else, my friends and Pete, is older than me so I keep winding them up, going, "I'm still in my twenties," while I still can.'

She had spoken about the possibility of adoption before and that was also still on the cards. 'I saw a horrific documentary on orphans in Bulgaria and it really affected me,' she revealed. 'I've got to get out there and help these children. It devastated me – I just wanted to bring some of them home. If I knew how to do it, I would do it tomorrow, but you have to wait years sometimes. I haven't had enough kids; I've got to have more. It feels more complete with a girl in the family, and Pete says Princess melts his heart, but I'm still very broody.'

In the event, Pete's present for Katie's thirtieth birthday

was another horse, called Dana. Katie has always been passionate about horses, but her interest was deepening still. She was now spending a great deal of time with the horsey set and there were even rumours that she wanted to compete in the Olympics. And, even if she didn't get that far, she was certainly upping her game; in June 2008, she competed in an event at Hickstead, finishing a very respectable sixth out of 27 competitors.

Katie had been riding since the age of seven, but this was the first such event she'd ever taken part in and she clearly loved it. 'I really enjoyed it. I've got a rosette, which is really good for me,' she said. 'I didn't come here to win it; I just wanted to participate. You've got to start somewhere.'

Indeed you do. And Katie had been working hard in preparation for this new side to her life, having daily dressage lessons for three months now, with a trainer called Andrew Gould. If Pete was concerned that this was set to pull them apart, however, he didn't show it publicly. But, behind the scenes, the couple were steadily, but inexorably moving apart.

Katie did what she always did on the back of a new development in her life: she turned it to her commercial advantage by signing up to put her name to a range of dressage products. It took her mind off the couple's chat show, which was axed in the autumn of 2008, but then they hadn't been counting on it too much – Katie and Pete were not obvious chat-show hosts. They did, however, sign up for another reality-TV series, *The Next Chapter*, which would reveal an awful lot more about them than they had initially thought.

Much as Katie was enjoying her new horsey life, however, there were still setbacks. In July 2008, she was mortified when it emerged publicly that she'd been refused entry to the VIP tent at the Cartier International Polo contest in Windsor. Worse still, when she offered to buy a £6,000 table for ten in the Chinawhite tent, she was turned down. It was a very public snub. 'It's a big shock and Kate's incredibly upset,' said her agent Claire Powell. 'We can only assume someone has it in for Katie.'

Katie herself was livid, and made no bones about it either, accusing the organisers of snobbery, saying that her glamour-model past embarrassed them and pointing out that she'd already met the Queen and Prince Charles (unlike a lot of the other attendees). She was absolutely right and the country came down very much on her side. Both Cartier and Chinawhite declined to comment on the situation.

Pete was also angry on her behalf. 'I am protective,' he said. 'It is a bit upsetting, because Kate's really got her heart set on horses. It's the one thing I know she's more passionate about than anything – as a hobby, as a first love. But Katie manages to do something no one else can do – she gets more publicity not turning up somewhere. Unbelievable.'

It wasn't long, though, before Katie got her revenge in the

most spectacular style: she was asked to perform a dressage routine before a military display by the Royal Household Cavalry for the diamond jubilee of the Horse Of The Year Show. It took a lot to make her appear like an excited teenager, but that was just how she came across now.

'Ever since I can remember, I've dreamed of riding at the Horse Of The Year Show, so I'm really excited at being asked to perform there,' she said of riding her horse, Glamour Girl. 'I know I'm not of the same standard as those riding there competitively, but I'm working with my trainer on something that will have a definite "wow" factor – and I can't wait.'

To add to her excitement, Charles Owen, riding-hat maker to the Queen, had sent her a bespoke hat. 'They sent me a lovely pink one and a black one,' Katie revealed. 'It's one of the nicest gifts I've ever been sent – they make the best hats in the world.'

Shortly afterwards, a personal invitation to the Gatcombe Horse Trials, held at Princess Anne's Gloucestershire estate, followed from BGC, Zara Phillips's sponsors. 'We invited Katie to Gatcombe because of her enthusiasm and love of horses and the strides she is making in equestrianism,' said James Blackshaw of BGC. 'We applaud her efforts.'

The general feeling in the horsey set was also clear: Katie loved riding and was a good horsewoman. To have been excluded from the Cartier event seemed somewhat over-grand.

The point was hammered home yet again when the British Equestrian Foundation named Katie as the face of Hoof, a campaign to inspire a generation of inner-city children to learn how to ride in the run-up to the Olympics. One snub was leading to an awful lot of solidarity from the rest of the horsey world. 'Some people may think horse riding is only available to a select few, but Katie's interest in riding and her open determination to do well at dressage are just the messages we want to give young people today,' said Barbara Cassani, head of the Games and also the woman instrumental in securing London's hosting of the Games.

Still, however, in public, no one seemed to notice quite how different Katie and Pete's worlds were now. Indeed, in some ways there seemed to be a return to business as usual, when the family jetted off to the States in August. Katie was to have yet another operation on her breasts (she hadn't been satisfied with the last one), while Pete was there to work on an album. And the cameras were there, as ever, with Pete musing that they sometimes shouldn't be quite so steamy in something that was to be shown on the television screens. 'But that's part of our life,' he told one interviewer. 'If someone's going to put a camera on you for 24 hours, they're gonna get you being moody, they're gonna get you being happy, they're gonna get quite a few emotions, and one of them's horny. Though when you're married, it's not every day you get horny, is it?'

It was yet another ominous note.

Katie, meanwhile, was appearing to be more horse-mad than ever. 'I have the Horse Of The Year Show coming up and I'm going to buy a horse now and aim for the Olympics,' she revealed on an interview with Lorraine Kelly on breakfast television. 'I went to the Burghley Horse Show the other week, which you could say is rather snobby, but they were really welcoming.' She didn't spell it out, but other, rather less welcoming institutions could clearly go hang.

Despite this new horsey existence, however, Katie couldn't quite let go of the old ways. She'd always been keen on a spat, not just with Pete, but with any other celebrity who riled her as well, and she took the opportunity of a new fragrance launch, Besotted, to really lash out. A few other celebrities had scents out at the same time, including one particular old foe. 'I didn't want the perfume launch to be boring like Victoria Beckham's, Kelly Brook and the others,' said Katie, looking as if butter wouldn't melt in her mouth, as she pranced around in a white basque and thong. The two new breasts were holding up well.

'I saw Victoria in pictures wearing the white dress with a kind of furry thing on the back and I just thought, She's on another night out. I had no idea she was supposed to be promoting her new perfume. She should have a bit more fun with it like I did. I envisaged a beach with a half-naked lady, and that's what I did. Now everyone has seen my new boobs and I hope I've made the public happy.'

Another bête noir was Kerry Katona, Katie's former friend and bridesmaid. Katie had publicly criticised Kerry's husband, Mark Croft, and Kerry was now threatening to write a book about her friend.

'How she can write anything about me is a joke,' said Katie. 'We met at the jungle and then did two photoshoots after that, and possibly met a couple of times out of work. But that was a long time ago and she doesn't know anything about my life. It's sad. I hear Kerry needs the money, but she shouldn't show off and splash money on things she can't afford.'

By this time, the importance of her equestrian life was becoming increasingly clear. In October, the Horse Of The Year Show took place: Katie took part in a masterclass, in conjunction with international competitor Henry Boswell and Andrew Gould. But it didn't go quite so well as her previous outing – Glamour Girl tried to skit across the ring, but Katie maintained her usual positive stance.

'At least I didn't fall off,' she announced. 'A lot of people mock me, but, until I started this, nobody had read about dressage.' As for the Olympics – 'Why ever not?' she stated. 'I'm not mad enough to do eventing, but myself and Andrew think dressage is possible. Never, ever underestimate the Price.'

In fact, by this stage, few were. The empire continued to

grow, encompassing books, scent, make-up, clothing, personal appearances and a huge amount more. The only element that frequently seemed to be missing was Pete, who clearly found the brave new world of dressage, in which his wife was now spending so much time, totally alien. Katie, meanwhile, continued to use her huge profile to speak out against animal abuse, particularly where it concerned horses, a subject increasingly close to her heart.

But where was Pete in all this? He had no role in the horsey side of her life and, by the autumn of 2008, rumours were rife that he didn't have much of a role elsewhere either. Katie admitted to a massive row in which she walked out for two days. Both had been seen out partying without the other in attendance.

By October, there was a sense that something was really wrong, with Pete apparently cancelling a recording session. 'Peter is feeling miserable because he is constantly fighting with Katie,' said a friend. 'Last weekend, he walked out on her and went to stay at his brother's apartment for a few days. He came back because he missed the kids, but things have been terrible since Wednesday. Peter doesn't want to go away while they aren't getting on, so he's concentrating on his marriage.'

Katie herself was scathing about the speculation. She'd been pictured out and about without Pete on a couple of occasions, but, after all, that did not mean the marriage had broken down, nor indeed, at that stage, that it was

The next step for Katie and Peter was to try to conquer the USA.

Above: They arrive at Heathrow with their mountain of luggage en route to America to promote *When Jordan Met Peter*.

Below: Their temporary home in Beverly Hills during the trip.

Above left: Katie, pregnant with her third child Princess Tiáamii, and Peter hit the shops in LA.

Above right: Katie, with her newborn little Princess, causes a storm as she arrives in Australia.

Bottom left: Peter and Katie clean up nicely for the Cosmopolitan Fun Fearless Female Awards.

Bottom right: They meet with US gossip blogger Perez Hilton in LA while filming their reality TV show, *Katie and Peter: Stateside.*

Above: Their gorgeous pink villa in Cyprus.

Below: Their Surrey mansion, purchased in 2008.

Katie and Peter accepted 'substantial damages' over a *News of the World* article that implied they were bad parents.

Family is always a priority for Katie and Peter.

Above left: With Princess Tiáamii and Junior.

Above right: With Harvey.

Below: Mega-business woman Katie brings her son and daughter to the launch of her new line of bed linen.

Above: Katie and Peter's appearance on *The Paul O'Grady Show* in April 2009, only a few weeks before the split, gave no indication that the couple were having problems and they even announced they were trying for another child.

Right: Training for the London Marathon in Malibu, California.

Katie and Peter draped in an American flag at the launch for their new reality TV show, in which they relocate their family to Malibu.

Katie and Peter tackled the 2009 Flora London Marathon on the 26 April, 2009. Even though Katie injured her knee (*bottom right*), they both completed the marathon in just over seven hours.

necessarily going to do so. 'I've only been pictured on a night out twice without Pete,' she said in one interview. 'Everyone assumes we're arguing and about to break up. Just because I went out two weeks on the trot with the girls, it's a big drama and everyone jumps to the conclusion we have split up. No one looks back to see when was the last time I went out without Pete – they just focus on one or two pictures and jump to conclusions. Pete and I laugh about it; we can't win. If we're smiling for the cameras, they say we're setting it up to gloss over the cracks. If we're not together, they think we've split up.'

Certainly, at that stage the couple were prepared to make a go of it. They renewed their wedding vows in South Africa, something that was captured on their reality-TV show, shortly after which Katie was named Britain's Best-loved Celebrity Mum. Her spirited and public defence of Harvey after he'd been mocked by *Heat* had made the public warm towards her even more, along with her ongoing desire to have an even bigger brood. There was also something more to cheer about when Princess Tiáamii, at the age of sixteen months, landed her first solo photoshoot. Naturally, Katie was delighted. It was, after all, a chip off the old block.

'She's going to be on the cover of *Prima Baby*, modelling party dresses,' announced Katie proudly. 'I'd like to get her and Junior into modelling – I think most parents would probably like to get their kids into modelling. I might put nail varnish on her and I was putting a bit of lipgloss on her for the shoot, but that was just messing about and I took it straight off afterwards because I don't agree with kids her age wearing make-up.'

Despite everything, rumours of problems in the marriage just would not go away. Although neither said so at that stage, their sex life was certainly not what it had been in the early days, and hints of that came through, even though the bigger problems were still in the background.

'He's a man and he will always want more sex than he gets,' Katie revealed at one stage. 'Pete might not get it often... but, when he does, it's worth it. We're just like any other married couple with three kids. I'm so honest.

'If I'm in a bad mood, I'm in a bad mood and I don't mind letting people know – it's a reality show, so I don't want it set up. And I probably look like I do moan, but what woman doesn't? That's what we are and we're no different off-camera to what we are on. It must look like we work all the time but I don't work as hard as a mum who has a nine-to-five job, so we don't have as much stress as people think, and Pete and I get to spend lots of time with our kids – we're very lucky.'

What Katie might not have realised herself at that point was that, courtesy of the reality-TV show, the public were actually watching a marriage breaking down. Lack of sex and constant rows become extremely wearing after a while and the fact that it was the same off-screen as on just made it more obvious that the strains were growing by the day. But not only did the couple themselves not want to admit what was happening to them, nor did the country as a whole. There was still enormous goodwill surrounding the two of them and the belief was palpable that somehow they would make it work.

There was also a good deal of admiration for Katie about her openly stated next aim: to win an Olympic gold. It seemed unlikely, but why not? Her determination was such that she'd achieved pretty much everything else that she'd set out for, so why not this too? 'It is a dream,' she admitted towards the end of 2008. 'I know I've only got a slim chance, but it's something I've got to aim for. There are thousands of brilliant riders out there. I know I might not make it, but I'll still give it a try. I have just bought another horse in Holland – it's one of the best in the world. You can pay up to six figures for the best. I'm loving it, and ride every day.

'Pete and I are going to the US in January for three months to film the next series of our reality show. I want to take one of my horses as I'll need to train. I've paid a lot of money for my horses – it's the same as if you race cars. You'd buy a Ferrari, not a Mini, and it's the same with dressage. I've bought the Rolls-Royce of horses.'

Nor had she forgotten that recent snub, which had also ended up endearing her to the public. 'If Cartier invited me next year, I wouldn't go – I'd never go now,' she said defiantly. 'I don't forget things like that – I won't even wear Cartier now. It's the sort of thing that has happened to me before, like when I was starting out and wanted certain people to manage me. They wouldn't because they dismissed me as just another Page 3 girl. Now they're kicking themselves because I'm doing well, and approaching me. I'm like, "Jog on.com." I have really good management around me. I've been asked to play in a polo match, which opens the Horse Of The Year Show. They have a celebrity on each side and I'm going to do that – it's bigger than the Cartier polo event.'

Despite all the emphasis on horses, however, Katie and Pete just could not convince the world that all was well. Rumours of a potential rift continued to grow and, no matter how much the couple protested, they still couldn't stamp them out. Katie was keen to talk about what attracted them most to each other: 'Pete loves me most with no make-up and wearing sweat pants and T-shirts,' she said. 'He fell in love with me in the jungle in *I'm A Celebrity*... and that's how he likes me to look.'

As for the marriage itself, everyone involved was adamant that all was well. 'I laugh when people say we don't get on,' revealed Katie. 'Of course we row, but we're best friends as well as partners. I don't think we'd know what to do without each other. People think my life is all about work and partying, but my favourite times are when we're all at home sitting in front of the telly or eating dinner together. Peter and I are in love and we are best mates. We row, we fight, we laugh, we call each other names, but we're exactly alike. We even try to match each other with what we wear. If I'm in white and he's not, he'll change. I know it's ridiculous, but it's just what we're like.'

But, of course, there was more to it than that. As later became apparent, they had all but stopped having sex by then, while, behind the scenes, Katie seemed to be putting Pete down. That might not have been her intention, but it was increasingly how she came across – not least to Pete, as well as everyone else.

Just before Christmas, there was another dash to hospital: to look after Harvey, who had come down with the flu. His disabilities meant he reacted more strongly to the virus than he might otherwise have done and so required extra medical care. The couple handled it as they always had done in the past – they simply got on with it.

But they weren't getting on with a great deal else. In interviews, Katie kept joking about the quiet state of their sex life, again seemingly not realising that this was on the verge of becoming a real problem for Pete. 'We do want another four kids,' she said on one occasion. 'I seem to conceive really easily; that's the trouble. It's probably why Pete doesn't get sex very much because I know what happens when he does. I know that'll be it – another baby!'

She also addressed the fact that both had been seen on

nights out without the other in tow. 'This year has been great,' said Katie firmly. 'Pete and I are getting on the best we ever have. I know we bicker a lot and wind each other up, but that's just the way we are. The other night we were watching re-runs of *I'm A Celebrity...* – the one when we met – even then we were picking on each other, like we do now. I see us being together for ever. He's my lover and my best friend. I get on with his family and he gets on with mine. He's bloody gorgeous as well! I know he's always complaining that he never gets enough sex, but, when he does get it, it's the best quality!'

There it was again – that lack of sex. Katie either wouldn't – or couldn't – see what a problem it was, though, and put it down to other people enjoying putting the couple down. 'There are always silly rumours. Like the one that I'm depressed because I've got acne,' she said. 'I haven't – it's a load of bollocks. I don't feel the pressure. I don't care what people say about how I look. I don't think I'm glamorous; I scrub up OK. I get knocked for what I do, but I'm lucky I seem to appeal to a lot of people. I don't know whether men fancy me any more. I'm not in the *FHM* Sexiest Women lists or anything. As long as Pete fancies me, I'm happy.'

Another issue was Katie's weight. She was looking slimmer than ever – and, once the split was announced, the pounds fell off her – but she was adamant there was nothing wrong there, either. 'I've never had a weight issue,' she said. 'Pete is obsessed with cooking pasta! Or we get Thai or curry takeaways, or have roast lamb, if I can be bothered to cook it! I love eating. We're having Christmas at home this year. All the family are coming over. I'm cooking gammon and Mum's doing a turkey. We wake up, unwrap our presents, go for a walk, play games and then veg out after eating lunch. I love it. I've put the tree up and been wrapping presents. I have to put the batteries in Harvey's presents before I wrap them because he gets frustrated if he can't play with them straight away.'

Motherhood had certainly mellowed her, with the arrival of Princess another cause for joy. 'I love having a daughter!' enthused Katie. 'She's such a girlie girl. She looks for pictures of me in the papers, and points and says, "Mummy, Mummy!" My kids are so used to my fame they probably think it's normal.'

It was a charming and domestic note on which to end the year. But 2008 was to be the last full year that Katie and Pete would be together. They were to start out full of hopes, with a short-term relocation to LA on the cards and the potential for breaking America, but, before the year was halfway through, they had announced their final split. The fairytale was about to end.

CHAPTER THIRTEEN
COAST TO COAST

Next stop: LA, but it wasn't going to be for long. Katie and Pete had signed up to run the London Marathon in April 2009, and so the trip to America was seen very much as dipping a toe in the water to test it out, after their earlier venture to introduce their show to the American public. Even so, the couple were greatly excited: they signed a four-month lease on a six-bedroom house in the same gated community in which Britney Spears lived, and set off. Some amusement was generated when they were seen at the airport with nineteen pieces of luggage: no one was talking about travelling light.

Initially, Katie was enthusiastic about the joys of it all. There was a big British expat community already out there, celebrities like Katie and Pete who spent time on both sides of the pond, and the full-time celebrity set, with whom Katie and Pete already had more than a passing acquaintance.

'I popped into Paris's birthday party two weeks ago,' Katie told one interviewer shortly after the couple had set up their new home. 'I met her a couple of years ago at the World Music Awards and we've stayed in touch. She's great. It was at her Beverly Hills home, which was pretty impressive. It was an amazing bash. Oh, and I saw her pink Bentley in the driveway. That's the car I want next – Pete's already got a black one.

'We chatted with Gordon Ramsay and his wife Tana at Elton John's post-Oscar party. They're a really fun couple. I like them because they banter with each other and have a laugh, like Pete and I do.' It was an ironic observation, in hindsight, for it was not long before the Ramsays were revealed as having had marital problems of their own.

At the same time, however, the couple were making plans for what would turn out to be their last high-profile venture together: the London Marathon. Katie and Pete were doing it for charity: having experienced first hand with Harvey the problems encountered by visually impaired children, they were attempting to raise £280,000 for the NSPCC and Vision. Katie was already making plans. 'On the day I'll probably be running with a photo of Harvey on my vest, which will provide a constant source of motivation,' she said. 'When I first started training I couldn't even run 200 metres, and Pete couldn't manage more than a mile; it was pretty daunting. But now we're both up to 13 miles and recently completed our first half-marathon.'

Even here, they were not immune from sniping from the rest of the world, however. 'People have been saying we've been posing for pictures in our running gear, jogging for two minutes and then turning back,' Katie continued. 'That is rubbish – I can't wait to prove my doubters wrong. I'm giving everything to this and have been training nearly every day – I can't even drink any more because it affects my training so much. I've become so boring since starting all of this – we both have! I'm a total lightweight now!'

Of course, Pete would have been delighted by this. Neither he, nor indeed Katie, ever made any secret of the fact that he didn't like her drinking, and so this healthy lifestyle, very much in keeping with the world of LA, would have gone down a treat with him. And he had plans of his own. Often accused of living in Katie's shadow, Pete had resumed his recording career and was getting on with work.

'I love it over here and have really been able to knuckle down and get on with the album,' he said. 'Running along the beach and seeing dolphins diving in and out of the waves is also a bit different to wrapping up in sub-zero conditions and running against the wind along Brighton Pier! I've lost over a stone and a half in weight since I started training and want to get really ripped by the day of the Marathon. We're both still eating absolute crap, though, so we're seeing a specialist nutritionist who's taking our body fat percentages and giving us an eating plan. It's so easy to be fit and look after yourself properly out here. I love it.'

Of course, the climate would have suited him – Pete did grow up in Australia, after all – but it was more than that. The easy-going, laidback lifestyle matched his easy-going character, and there was, perhaps, a simplicity in the life they led that they didn't have back in the UK. Nor were they so constantly snapped by the cameras – except those filming their latest reality-TV show – which gave them a sense of greater freedom than before. People really didn't know who they were – ironically, of course, this was to lead to the row caught on camera that signalled the death knell of the relationship – and this again allowed them a little more peace. The only trouble was, Katie didn't enjoy it anything like as much as her husband did. She relished the limelight and, although her personality matched the American make-something-of-your-life ideal, she simply didn't take to the lifestyle in the same way that Pete did. That, however, had not yet become quite clear.

Now that she was a respectable married woman, she sometimes regretted her early years. Interviewed on television by Piers Morgan, Katie admitted she particularly regretted her fling with former *Pop Idol* Gareth Gates, when she was pregnant with Harvey.

However, at the same time, her words showed up a vulnerability and a need for stability clearly still there. That her own marriage was on the verge of failing made it doubly ironic: Katie did indeed go on to attain what she had needed back then, but it was about to fall apart. 'When I look at it now, it's gross, disgusting,' she said. 'It's terrible – I was still young, I was pregnant, I didn't have the dad about and I still wanted to be loved. It was wrong when I look back. It was over in seconds!'

She also spoke openly about the most hurtful rumours she'd had to contend with, those concerning her oldest child. She had been frequently informed that her own party lifestyle might have been the reason for his problems, but this was something she staunchly denied. 'You're told your child is blind and then you're called the Mother from Hell,' she said. 'It was hurtful. People would look at me and I knew they were thinking, It's her fault he's like that. It's not easy; he's challenging. But that's my life and I wouldn't change it for anything.' Unfortunately, of course, change was now just a few short months away.

Another unfortunate episode in Katie's life around that time concerned Jade Goody. Sadly, the reality-television star was by now nearing the end of her fight with cancer, and very publicly saying goodbye to the world. Katie had never held back when she'd had an opinion about anything, and so had criticised Jade for being so very open about her illness. Jade had responded in turn by calling her a 'hypocrite', not least because Katie had in the past spoken of her own brush with cancer, in the growth on her hand.

Now that Jade was on the verge of death, however, it seemed that Katie was regretting her somewhat harsh words. Jade had made no bones about the fact that she was doing everything she could to provide for her children's future. Katie was also a mother, of course, and recognised fellow maternal feeling when she saw it. 'When I come back, the first thing I'm going to do is go to Jade's and say goodbye,' she said. 'It's something I want to do in private, away from the cameras. I don't know what I'll say, but, whatever it will be, will be between me and her.'

In the end, it was a reconciliation that was never to take place.

After the couple had been in the States for a few months, rumours began to emerge that all was not well. There had been speculation over the true state of the marriage for months now, of course, and added to that were increasing reports that Katie was not happy with her new life in the States. In some ways, that made sense. At the heart of it, underneath all the glamour, the celebrity, the years spent as Jordan, the drinking, the nightclubs and the men, Katie was fundamentally a country girl from Sussex who loved horses. Yes, her life had become very different from the one she was brought up to, and, yes, she loved being rich and famous, too, but sometimes it takes a stint in another country to tell you who you really are, and Katie was beginning to realise that she didn't want the States to be her permanent home.

But it's not at all clear if she was ready to admit that even to herself back then. Katie was nothing if not a trouper, and believed in putting on a brave face to the world, and so she did what she always did. She got on with it, pooh-poohed the rumours in public and tried to make the best of it behind the scenes. 'Everyone's been showing me all these stupid gossip magazines which are all saying I'm depressed, I'm on painkillers, I'm not eating, me and Pete are splitting up – it's ridiculous,' she told one interviewer. 'I find it all laughable.

'You know Pete and I – you've seen for yourselves how we are together away from the cameras, and you know it's not an act. We do bicker, but that's just the way we are – we enjoy it!

'I love Pete, bless him. I really do. I've just had a tattoo of his name engraved on to my left wrist, which no one knows about yet. I had it done in Las Vegas as a surprise. He's already got my name on his ring finger, so I thought it only fair. If we were on the verge of splitting up, would I really bother going through the pain of getting a tattoo done?'

Of course, Katie didn't realise the relationship was near breaking point – the final decision came from Pete. Nor did she realise that their lack of a sex life continued to take its toll. She was still cracking jokes about it, at one point saying, 'After the Marathon, he's going to get lucky this year, for the first time, so I can 100 per cent guarantee that I will be pregnant sometime this year.' Sadly, this was not to be.

Pete himself was still making jokes about it, though. The couple were back in Britain in the run-up to the Marathon, and they still seemed outwardly normal, although Pete was determined that they should resume the life they'd had before.

'We've been absolutely knackered for the past few weeks,' he said. 'So there are two main reasons I want to complete the run: one, because it's for charity and, two, because we can get back to normal action in the bedroom. Kate's promised it'll happen on Sunday night, but I'm guessing she'll be pretty knackered after all that running. Even if she's not, I might not be fit for it! But thank God our sex life should be back on track pretty soon – I can't wait!'

But why so out of kilter in the first place? Admittedly, the couple had three small children to look after, and Katie had been open about suffering from depression, but, even so, the lack of passion was a sure sign that something was going badly wrong. Nor is it often a good idea to designate a night when everything returns to normal in a relationship, because, not only does it build up expectation that might not be fulfilled, it also doesn't tackle the underlying cause as to what is wrong. Perhaps even now, at this very late stage, the relationship could have been saved if they'd made a super-human effort – but, in actual fact, they were reaching the moment of self-destruct.

Katie and Pete, though, were doing their best to look to the future. 'I'm definitely going to get pregnant this year,' said Katie. 'We want another child; we don't care if it's a boy or girl. We haven't thought about names yet, either, but I'm sure that's one thing we'll start talking about as soon as I'm pregnant.'

But, of course, you can't get pregnant without sex – and both of them had been perfectly open about the fact that it had not been on the agenda for an awfully long time.

In an interview just before the Marathon, Katie made a highly revealing remark, and one that provided the clue as to why it all went so badly wrong. When their relationship was going well, it was because they were operating as a team. However, when they started trying to get one up on each other, it all turned sour. 'We are not competing with each other this time,' Katie said. 'I want to make sure I'm crossing the finishing line with Pete because we want to enjoy it together after all that training. It'd be romantic if he carried me over the finishing line, but we're not allowed. Everybody has to run over it. We didn't get on each other's nerves much at all in the build-up to the Marathon. To be honest, it's been great having Peter around to keep me going. When it gets hard, we're always there to make the other one keep going. If we were on our own, we might have just given up or got lazy, but it went really well working together.'

'I wouldn't leave her,' said Pete (referring to running the actual race). 'I have to make sure she's OK and enjoying herself.'

That reference to not competing with one another this time round made it crystal clear, of course, that that was exactly what they'd done in the past. And perhaps it was because Katie had always had to compete so hard to get to where she was, at the top of the showbusiness tree, that she simply couldn't see that this was a recipe for disaster where Pete was concerned. And it is sadly ironic that it was only now, when the end was near, that the couple had managed to train together without that competitive edge reappearing. But, by this time, it was all far too late.

The presence of the recently deceased Jade Goody still hung over them. Katie had never managed to make it up with her, and so it was perhaps for this reason that Pete wanted to show some memento of her when he ran. 'I said I would do this when the news first emerged her cancer was terminal,' he said. 'I can't believe such a lovely young woman has died in such a tragic way. I always liked Jade. She was a good girl right from back in the day; she was in the same sort of industry as us, and it really brings it home how these awful things can happen.

'Cancer is such a horrible disease and I just wanted to remember Jade somehow during the Marathon. She doesn't have a specific charity yet so we couldn't donate to that, but we would have, if we could. The only good thing that came from her death was that it raised awareness for the disease. She could really become a bit of a hero by letting other young women know about cervical cancer, and maybe save their lives.'

On a more positive note, both were upbeat about the physical benefits of running the Marathon, although Katie was as self-critical as ever. 'I don't like my muscles at all,' she admitted. 'I'm still really thin, but all the muscles in my legs are quite bulked up and they're not very attractive. It's really unfeminine. I just hope they'll fade quickly, because I want to get back to my proper figure asap.'

Pete was altogether more pleased. 'Long-distance running doesn't slim you down,' he said. 'It's just turned everything to muscle, so I'm pretty much the same size and weight I was. But now I'm going to get into proper training, with sprinting and weight lifting to get really ripped and toned again. I had a great body when I was younger and I want to try and head in that direction again. I'm 36 now and I'd love to prove to myself I could do it.'

In the event, Katie and Pete pulled it off, making it across the finishing line in a respectable 7 hours and 11 minutes. 'I am absolutely over the moon,' said Katie, who was on the verge of tears. 'My knee was hurting, but there was no way I was going to stop.'

Pete was similarly chuffed, but it was one of the last times that the two of them would be seen out together. Behind the scenes, matters had got too much: the marriage had irrevocably broken down. The rows, the lack of sex and the competition between the two had become too great, and it was Pete, arguably the far more laidback one of them, who decided that he had finally had enough. For all the happiness family life had brought him, he simply couldn't take the stresses and strains any more, and he certainly couldn't handle it when pictures were published of his wife looking as if she was canoodling with another man.

And so it was, unaware that Pete had finally had enough, that Katie put in place what would be the catalyst for the breakdown of the marriage. She, and a group of fellow horse-mad enthusiasts, decided to go out for a night on the tiles. The couple had just run the Marathon together, but now they were running in totally different directions, away from a fairytale that had started in the jungle and enchanted the world.

CHAPTER FOURTEEN
SEPARATE LIVES

The split was final: that much was clear. When the problems between the couple first surfaced, there were some hopes that they might be able to stage a form of reconciliation, but it was not to be. A glum Katie returned from her break in the Maldives. Meanwhile, Pete was back from Cyprus, but no longer at the couple's mansion in Woldingham, Surrey. Matters were looking grim.

Indeed, insiders had been shocked at how the situation had worsened so quickly. Any early hopes that this might be an amicable parting were dashed, but then at that point no one realised quite how long there had been problems in the marriage and quite how deep they were. However, the problem of the children was what was on everyone's mind.

'Pete has no interest in discussing his financial rights,' said a friend. 'His sole priority is his children and Harvey.

Both Kate and Pete want the divorce to be amicable, but it is still very early days and things have already turned far nastier than anyone could have ever predicted. Pete's a great dad and wants regular access to his kids, which means joint custody. He is praying Kate appreciates this and doesn't block the move. It is so rare for a father to be granted sole custody, but, if Kate was to go off the rails, then clearly this is what he would push for. It's not about the money – he doesn't want to profit from divorce. He'll come out only with what he put into their three-and-a-half-year marriage, but it is still an incredibly messy situation and deeply unpleasant.'

Neither side appeared to be able to see reason. Peter was, however, pictured playing with the two younger children on Brighton beach, with both children clearly happy to be with their dad.

'I am OK now I'm with my babies,' he told a journalist afterwards. 'It's been a really tough couple of weeks, but being with them is the best tonic in the world. It makes everything better. I missed them so much when they were away from me – it was by far the worst part of what has happened. But today has helped me to forget all the negative stuff. All I want now is to have a fun day with them. I am going to get to see Harvey, which will be absolutely fantastic. He is such a special boy and I haven't seen him, so I am looking forward to it more than you can imagine.'

At this point, it appeared that Katie was having second thoughts. There were reports that she'd texted her estranged husband, asking for a face-to-face meeting, a request Pete point-blank turned down. Given that both had now consulted lawyers, it was looking pretty unlikely that there would be a reconciliation anyway, and, in any case, Pete really had had enough.

Katie certainly seemed very torn. One minute she was telling friends she was moving on, the next she was reportedly saying, 'I'll take Pete back tomorrow. If only I could turn back the clock. I've made the biggest mistake of my life.'

But it didn't help that, despite this, she was still seen out riding, something that had led to one of the biggest bones of contention between them. The relationship was clearly doomed: Pete was said to be asking for a quickie divorce.

He might have wanted a divorce, but the effect on him of all that was happening was clear. He'd lost a huge amount of weight, and admitted to feeling like a 'zombie'. As friends pointed out, he came from a large Greek family, where the last thing anyone wants to think about is divorce. Katie, meanwhile, had been due to make an appearance on the *Jonathan Ross Show* to talk about the split, but at the last minute pulled out.

Harvey's seventh birthday rolled round: Pete gave him a £1,000 musical centre, but he didn't see the boy. Public opinion, however, seemed very much to be turning in his favour. He made his first public appearance since the announcement at a show held by male dance troupe Here Come The Boys! at the O2 Arena in London. While he didn't actually take part in the show himself, he was cheered by hundreds of women in the audience when he took to the stage.

'I'm very happy to be here,' Pete told them. 'I know how much effort these guys have put into the show. You've got great-looking guys out the back and you've got great-looking girls in the front.'

It was, at least, an indication that he felt he could appear in front of fans once more. He also found a new house to live in: in Hove, West Sussex, about 40 miles away from the family home.

But Pete wasn't the only one to have suffered a severe weight loss. Katie was booked to model at the Clothes Show London at ExCeL, showcasing her most recent KP equestrian range, and shocked onlookers with her gaunt appearance, highlighted by the fact that most of her ribcage was on display.

'Despite what people see while Katie is out, behind closed doors it is very different,' said a friend. 'She thinks she's been portrayed as the bad guy in her split from Pete and the pressure of this enormous backlash has really taken its toll.

'She's barely eating and reckons she's lost around 12lb in a relatively short space of time. For someone of her slight build, it's very noticeable. The stress of an impending divorce has given her sleepless nights and she has several work commitments to fulfil. Katie doesn't know who she can trust and feels she is public enemy number one. Behind the public bravado, she's in bits – both physically and mentally.'

Katie also received a rapturous reception from the crowd, in the form of a standing ovation, but it was all too much. She was supposed to have put in a second appearance later in the day, but didn't. The strain was really beginning to tell.

Of course, there was a huge amount of speculation about whether either of them had ever been unfaithful. Pete was adamant that he certainly hadn't been. 'I never once strayed from Kate,' he told friends. 'I was brought up to believe marriage was for life and this goes against everything my family and I stand for. Kate and I had our troubles like any other couple, but I never gave up until the very, very end.

'I would never walk away from the marriage without thinking about it long and hard; I didn't just up and fly the nest. I believe marriage is for life and this has left me utterly devastated.'

Matters were not helped when Katie was spotted out clubbing, flirting and grinding as she did so, with pictures all over the papers the next day. In fact, this was this kind of behaviour that was beginning to lose her public sympathy, not least as Pete had reportedly wanted to be with the children on the night in question, whereas they were left in the care of a nanny. Next, she was spotted at a Boyzone gig, looking the worse for wear. This might have been her way of coping, but it wasn't doing her any favours. 'We're obviously concerned for her and hope she gets through whatever troubles she has at the minute,' said Mikey Graham, singer with the band.

There were further reports that she had again asked Pete to take her back, but matters by now were totally out of control. Pete was, however, becoming more than a little concerned for her obvious distress. 'He knew she would be upset, but thought their marriage had run its natural course,' said a friend. 'He feels really bad about the whole situation as he cares for Katie deeply and hates to see her like this. All her desperate phone calls are really heartbreaking, but he's determined to stay strong. Deep down he knows that it's not right to get back together, no matter how much it's hurting Katie. In the long term, it's better for both of them.'

Meanwhile, Pete himself was miserable, in that he was only able to see the children at weekends, something that was tearing him apart. As it was revealed that the two had had marital therapy in an attempt to save the relationship, Pete said, 'The past four weeks have been the worst of my life. It was hell. No matter what happens, you never stop loving someone. Initially, I couldn't even have thought about work – my head was everywhere; it still is everywhere. But it's been a month now and I know I've got to start pulling myself together. The response I've had since being in China has been absolutely amazing. This, and the work I am doing now, is beginning to give me confidence again. Singing has given me something to focus on.'

Indeed, he had travelled to Macau, China, to sing at the Bollywood awards, and received a standing ovation just for his rehearsals. It clearly cheered him up. 'I never expected the attention I've been getting and I am so glad this is happening,' he said. 'I've only been here a couple of days, but it's already turned out better than I ever hoped. Finally, I am beginning to smile again. It's not like I'm a bundle of joy now, but it's getting better. I'm even cracking terrible jokes.'

No one was really having that much of a laugh, however. Katie was certainly going through terrible mood swings, as the full impact of what was happening made itself felt.

'Katie's hit rock bottom,' admitted a friend. 'She doesn't know what to do with herself; her behaviour is all over the place. She's been sobbing, trying to call Peter and attacking anyone she can. Her friends are worried she's drinking too much. [But] she's going to come back from this. I have never seen her so determined. She likes a fight and she wants to beat him.'

Then there was a bizarre interlude in which the singer Dane Bowers, Katie's ex, appeared to get involved. He was arrested on a drink-driving charge when a friend's car was found crashed into a hedge. Dane countered this by saying that he had actually been at Katie's at the time, at a party. It later emerged that two weeks previously he had split from his wife Chrissy Johnston and had been spending time with Katie.

Nor did it help that Peter wouldn't take her calls. 'He wouldn't pick up,' said the source. 'He's refusing to take her calls. She was in tears with frustration and sadness. Peter's lack of contact is driving Katie to distraction. She's been used to taking out her anger on Peter for years and, now that she can't, she doesn't quite know how to deal with it.

'She's complaining constantly, especially about not being able to sleep. She's become unbearable. She's finding it tough around the kids and isn't getting up and about until they've already left for school. She's spending most of the day lying in bed, bossing people about. She's very moody.' It was, of course, exactly the kind of behaviour that had been instrumental in driving Pete away.

And so it ended as it had begun: as a competition. When the two of them entered the jungle, the aim was to come first. That aim, certainly for Katie, never really went away. But the great irony was that, having had a number of boyfriends who treated her badly, in Pete she really had found a kind, honourable family man. As with so many people who don't always appreciate what they have underneath their noses, she perhaps didn't realise that. But then Katie might well be simply unable to trust anyone: her earliest experiences with men were unpleasant, and, although she had publicly stated that she had put those things behind her, perhaps the longer-term effect was that she would be unable ever to see men in a totally flattering light.

Both Katie and Pete showed themselves to be brave in that jungle, but, ultimately, their relationship would not survive the jungle that is celebrity life. There is no question about the fact that they loved one another, but what had started out as a fairytale simply ended in bitterness and tears. Theirs was a life and a romance lived out in public: the meeting, the wedding and the numerous reality-TV shows they made trumpet all that, but, all too often, passion burns itself out and theirs had done so. Ultimately, Katie and Pete were just too much in love.